Fine Lines

Fine Lines

The Talking Stick
Volume 26

A publication of the
Jackpine Writers' Bloc, Inc.
Menahga, Minnesota

www.thetalkingstick.com
www.jackpinewriters.com
Send correspondence to sharrick1@wcta.net or
Jackpine Writers' Bloc, Inc., 13320 149th Avenue,
Menahga, Minnesota 56464.

Cover photograph taken by Tarah L. Wolff
Managing Editors: Sharon Harris, Tarah L. Wolff
Copy Editors: Sharon Harris, Marilyn Wolff
Layout, Production and Cover Design: Tarah L. Wolff
Editorial Board: Marlys Guimaraes, Sharon Harris, Mike Lein,
        Marilyn D. Wolff, Tarah L. Wolff

List of Contributors

Beverly Abear	47
Pagyn Alexander	55
Olivia Anderson	160
Lina Belar	64
James Bettendorf	181
Louise Bottrell	43, 79
Mary Lou Brandvik	16
Janice Larson Braun	76, 150
Tim J. Brennan	6, 118
Stephanie Brown	177
Sue Bruns	54, 169
Judy Budreau	117
Sharon Chmielarz	140
Jan Chronister	128
Mary A. Conrad	183
Chet Corey	31, 83, 119, 185
Sarah Cox	122
Frances Ann Crowley	20
Dianne M. DelGiorno	53, 96
Norita Dittberner-Jax	109
Charmaine Pappas Donovan	7, 81, 138
Carol Dunbar	147
Virginia Eckert	38, 65
Larry Ellingson	179
Edis Flowerday	8
Marsha Foss	129, 142
Cindy Fox	25, 87, 110
Neil Millam Frederickson	69
M. K. Fuller	13
Katie Gilbertson	41

List of Contributors

Georgia A. Greeley	106, 114, 167
Annamae Gunsolus-Holzworth	105
Marlys Guimaraes	68, 151
Richard G. Hagen	163, 168
Kate Halverson	84
Laura L. Hansen	12, 127
Sharon Harris	24, 104, 113, 133, 143
Audrey Kletscher Helbling	46, 77, 131, 139, 145
Jennifer Hernandez	95, 100
Arnie Johanson	190
Charles Johnson	35, 153
Christina Joyce	2
Meridel Kahl	94, 130
Paisley Kauffmann	21
Karla Klinger	49
Norma Thorstad Knapp	17
Kathryn Knudson	97, 171, 186
Elisa Korenne	191
Janet Kurtz	161
David J. Laliberte	187
Kim A. Larson	125
Kristin Laurel	32, 137
Mike Lein	111
Brianna Liestman	193
Renee Loehr	164
Dawn Loeffler	85
Linda Maki	115
Cheyenne Marco	4, 29, 51
Dan McKay	32
Susan McMillan	67, 86

List of Contributors

René Bartlett Montgomery	146, 175
Michael Kiesow Moore	59
Marcia Neely	165
Ryan M. Neely	157
Joni Norby	154
David Eric Northington	34
Andrew O'Kelley	91
Alberta Lee Orcutt	27, 33
Ronald j. Palmer	56
Yvonne Pearson	135
Susan Perala-Dewey	116
Alan Perry	121
Adrian S. Potter	66, 73
Deborah Rasmussen	141
Kit Rohrbach	19
Lane Rosenthal	172
Deb Schlueter	101
Mary Schmidt	136
Ruth Schmidt-Baeumler	10, 178
Lisa M. Bolt Simons	107
Peter Stein	80, 134
Doris Stengel	124
Marlene Mattila Stoehr	60, 123
Carissa Jean Tobin	1
Alberta Tolbert	72
Peggy Trojan	149, 159
Steven R. Vogel	103
Beth L. Voigt	57
Susan Niemela Vollmer	28, 44
Kim-Marie Walker	61

List of Contributors

Justin Watkins	182, 189
Elizabeth Weir	40, 90
Bonnie West	155
Cheryl Weibye Wilke	89, 174
Florence Witkop	152
Marilyn D. Wolff	11
Tarah L. Wolff	39, 50, 144, 173
Kevin Zepper	45, 93
Darryl Zitzow	15

Co-Editor's Note – Sharon Harris
Editor's Choice: Mugs (p.193)
by Brianna Liestman

This year, my Editor's Choice is the poem "Mugs" by Brianna Liestman (p.193). This poem demonstrates such a humorous, simple way of defining human behavior and human relationships. The parallels drawn here are very clever. The last stanza especially spoke to me. I have been in relationships like this. I am so clearly here to stay, my decisions made, my solid and heavy ceramic mug showing that I have no intentions of leaving this state, this town, this job. And across from me sits a great love, but clearly he is ready to move on at an instant's notice, disposable cup, disposable job, no deep roots, his love not as solid as mine.

I have already learned that changing geography does not erase problems—they follow you wherever you go and you will still have to deal with them. And moving all over the country, with all the disruption of moving your family and the cost, rarely increases your income enough to be worth it. And then you are away from family and friends and roots and always spending money to come back to visit.

How sad this can be when two people really care about each other, but one has wanderlust and one has already found where they want to live and where they want to be. One of you would need to try to change in order for this to work. And is that fair? No, it's not, but compromise always seems to be needed.

I often use this space in my Editor's Note to remind writers how our procedures work each year. We are proud that we have been in existence for over twenty years. Last year, we put out our twenty-fifth book and had an especially large book and bigger book release party. This year, we tried something a little different, asking for shorter submissions. Even though we had that slight change this year, we still want to continue our quest to publish Minnesota writers or those with a strong connection to Minnesota. We like stories with a Northwoods flavor and we like to create a book with some heart-warming but still with sometimes a lesson-to-learn type of writing. After our March 1 deadline, then we have five of our members form as the Editorial Board so we can choose the poems and stories that we want in the book and we choose our top ones for honorable mention and possible prizes. Those of us on the Board of Directors or our Editorial Board are not eligible for the prizes. We have had outside impartial judges only for the job of selecting first and second places for the prize money from the top few submissions (with the writers' names removed). These judges have also been gracious enough to supply some helpful comments and suggestions on all of our chosen top submissions.

It is amazing, really, that our writers find something new to write about each year. Surely you would think that every possible thing had already been thought of, discussed to death, and written down many times. Each year, we love to see the new submissions, read and explore the work of new writers and see more work of returning writers that we have grown familiar with over the years.

We hope you all enjoyed the challenge of writing shorter, more concise submissions as much as we did.

Co-Editor's Note - Tarah L. Wolff
Editor's Choice: Driftwood One-Matcher (p.189)
by Justin Watkins

My editor's choice this year is a poem that fashions a picture of a place I can smell and touch and the poet does this in very few words. It may be that I myself love to camp and have yet to feel that I have had the opportunity to do it enough. When I was younger, I day dreamed and fantasized about a little wild place down a long low-maintenance road on a little lake with no name.

As I got older the dream reached to include my husband and the accommodations changed from a tent to a little one room cabin and an outhouse with a half moon on the door. What has always remained the same in this dream is that it is a wild place where no one else goes and the lake is small enough to be all mine and, now, all ours.

I can see my husband building the altar as the writer does for his son in this poem. An altar of wood taken from the surrounding trees and driftwood fetched from the shore. It is an altar of peace and comfort, an altar that offers an answer to the most primal of needs: heat on a cold night.

I know that when the sun goes down, and us humans are nothing but animals sharing a shore, and there is no man-made light to obstruct the sky, that it is a church. Our first church, that has no dress code, that is always open, that requires so little to return to and settle in to a pew to hear the opening choir of the loons across the lake. We will hold our hands to the flickering warmth of our altar and speak only in whispers so that we do not interrupt the service.

This year we reduced our word count for submissions dramatically and I found that it did nothing short of improving us as writers and I believe we even impressed ourselves with how few words we actually need.

Poetry
Judge: LouAnn Shepard Muhm

LouAnn Shepard Muhm is a poet and teacher from northern Minnesota. Her poems have appeared in *Antiphon, Alba, Red River Review, Eclectica, Pirene's Fountain*, and *CALYX*, among other journals and anthologies, and she was a finalist for the Creekwalker Poetry Prize and the Late Blooms Postcard Series. Muhm is a recipient of Minnesota State Arts Board Artist Initiative Grants in Poetry in 2006 and 2012, and has been featured twice in the "What Light" poetry sponsored by the McKnight Foundation and the Walker Art Museum. Her full-length poetry collection *Breaking the Glass* (Loonfeather Press, 2008) was a finalist for the Midwest Book Award in Poetry. Muhm was awarded an MFA in poetry from Sierra Nevada College in 2016.

Winner - Carissa Jean Tobin
the way we move (p. 1)

Carissa Jean Tobin teaches Spanish in Minneapolis. Her poem "Minneapolis at Large" was published in the *2014 Chinook Book*. Carissa's blog *Good Work, Great Life* and her website www.goodworkgreatlife.com both give tips for efficient living. Her hobbies include creating humorous surveys for friends and lounging at the café formerly known as Wilde Roast.

Second Place - Tim J. Brennan
Self Portrait (p.6)

Tim J. Brennan's poetry can be found in many places including *Green Blade, The Lake* (U.K.), *Talking Stick*, and *Sleet*. His one act plays have played across the country including stages in Rochester and White Bear Lake, MN, Colorado Springs, Milwaukee, and Gulf Shore, AL.

Creative Nonfiction
Judge: Marge Barrett

Marge Barrett has published a chapbook of poems, *My Memoir Dress*, and a memoir, *Called: The Making & Unmaking of a Nun*. Her work has appeared in numerous journals and is anthologized in Dzanc Books' *Best of the Web* and Minnesota Historical Society Press's *The State We're In*. Receiving an MFA in Creative Writing from the University of Minnesota, she has taught in high schools and colleges. Currently, she teaches classes at the Loft Literary Center in Minneapolis and conducts a variety of workshops.

Winner - Christina Joyce
An Italian Education (p.2)

Christina Joyce lives in St. Paul, MN, but often seeks writing inspiration in other parts of the world, particularly Italy, birthplace of her maternal grandparents. She has degrees in journalism and public administration, works as a government communicator, and feeds her creative muse in the writing communities at the University of Iowa and Loft Literary Center. Most recently, her work was published in the *2017 Saint Paul Almanac*.

Second Place - Charmaine Pappas Donovan
Another Kind of Bonanza (p.7)

Charmaine is a poet and writer from the Cuyuna Range and Brainerd Lakes area. Her writing is published in anthologies, journals, magazines, and newspapers. She is a member of local, state, and national literary organizations. She is currently the third Vice President, Special Awards Chair for the National Federation of State Poetry Societies, Inc.

Fiction
Judge: Rochelle Hurt

Rochelle Hurt is the author of two poetry collections: *In Which I Play the Runaway* (2016), which won the Barrow Street Book Prize, and *The Rusted City* (2014), published in the Marie Alexander Series in prose poetry from White Pine Press. She is the recipient of prizes and fellowships from *Crab Orchard Review, Arts & Letters, Hunger Mountain, Poetry International,* Vermont Studio Center, Jentel, and Yaddo. Her poetry, flash fiction, and creative nonfiction have appeared in journals like *Crazyhorse, Black Warrior Review,* and *The Southeast Review.* She holds an MFA from UNC Wilmington and a PhD from the University of Cincinnati. Currently, she teaches creative writing courses on poetry and short forms for Meredith College and the Loft Literary Center online.

Winner - Cheyenne Marco
Harvest (p.4)

Cheyenne Marco grew up on a Minnesota poultry farm and finds inspiration for her writing in her rural upbringing. She teaches at USD, does outreach for Friends of the Big Sioux River, and fantasizes about sleep. Her works have appeared in *Rathalla Review, Turk's Head Review,* and *Prairie Winds.*

Second Place - Edis Flowerday
Special Delivery (p.8)

Edis Flowerday writes short stories, has completed two thirty-minute screenplays, and is working on a novel. She has had stories published in *Lake Region Review* and *Talking Stick.* She produced *Date Night at the Boxwood: Thirteen Stories.* Ms. Flowerday lives in Minneapolis with her husband Larry Risser.

Honorable Mention
Chosen by our Editorial Board

Poetry
The Hovering Years (p.124) Doris Stengel
Midnight Blue (p.86) Susan McMillan
The Last Battle (p.181) James Bettendorf
Mugs (p.193) Brianna Liestman
Laundry and Reproach (p.127) Laura L. Hansen

Creative Nonfiction
Pressing Matters (p.161) Janet Kurtz
How Much She Had Lost (p.17) Norma Thorstad Knapp
Canned Cranberries (p.55) Pagyn Alexander
Waiting (p.169) Sue Bruns

Fiction
Art Obsession (p.139) Audrey Kletscher Helbling
The Odds (p.21) Paisley Kauffmann
Mistakes (p.87) Cindy Fox

This volume
of
The Talking Stick
is dedicated
to writer

Louise Bottrell
1937-2017

". . . the silent snows,
the rains in spring, then filtered sunlight,
blue violets and purple clover."

From "Visiting Abigail"
Published in *Talking Stick 15*

Fine Lines

Poetry – First Place
Carissa Jean Tobin

the way we move

There were infections in our backs and aches in our sinuses and our ears heard too much. We looked at the boxes and they didn't pack themselves. We looked at the couch and it didn't carry itself. We looked at our phones and they started calling for help. The helpers ate at Chipotle and packed bananas in boxes and found clothes we never should have bought. The rashes poisoned our food. We sat on the floor because the chairs were covered with books we'd never read and books we'd never sell and books we'd never write. We slept on the couch when the bed rolled itself away.

Creative Nonfiction – First Place
Christina Joyce

An Italian Education

It was Mom's idea to hop the train.

One moment we were two law-abiding American citizens waiting on the platform at the train station in Florence, the next we were scrambling across railroad tracks, bags swinging off our shoulders like a couple of hobos on the lam. A dozen other people were making the same mad dash to catch the 11:07 train to Venice, triggered by the announcement that our train had arrived, not where we were, but four tracks over. Since we had only two minutes before departure, we did what any desperate traveler would do: we jumped onto the tracks.

We had reason to be skittish around train stations after the incident in Rome the previous week. On that Saturday morning, the area outside the station hummed with teenagers loitering on steps, hucksters selling yellowed postcards, and beggar women with fake babies at their breasts, their real children scurrying around trying to pick our pockets. We skirted the sideshows and headed into the station.

As we neared the ticketing area, we heard a BOOM from deep within the station. I dismissed it as falling luggage until, seconds later, we saw a flash of light and heard another BOOM, followed by popping sounds. Smoke curled toward the entrance, overtaking the crowd as we rushed into the street. A woman in black, tottering on heels too high for running, cried, "O, Dio! O, Dio!"

We waited with hundreds of others as a dozen policemen entered the station, walking side by side with billy-clubs drawn. The chattering crowd seemed more annoyed than frightened by the incident. An Italian man explained that the blasts were caused by soccer fans who lit firecrackers and cherry bombs to protest the train delay to Florence. The police retaliated by tossing tear gas into the crowd.

"These people give our country such a bad name," the man said. He stared at the smoky entrance of the station one hundred yards away and described the state of the current Roman Empire. High unemployment and lack of prospects for Italy's youth have led to many disturbances such as this one, he said.

Now, a week later in Florence, we carried a new-found wariness of train stations and soccer fans. The new track was two hundred yards from us, the official way. Seeing a number of other travelers ignoring the posted signs to stay off the tracks, my sixty-seven-year-old mother nodded toward our train. "Let's take the shortcut," she suggested. I shrugged. *Why not? When in Florence, do as the Florentines do.*

Somehow we made it across the steel tracks and gravel bed without twisting an ankle or tumbling on our faces. Strong arms reached down to help Mom up the steep steps of the car, with an added boost from me below. I tossed our two suitcases up and clambered aboard.

After brushing the dust from our rumpled clothes, we turned around to thank our new friends—a car full of boisterous soccer fans.

Fiction – First Place
Cheyenne Marco

Harvest

I have to do it in the barn. Not that it's an ideal place. Even though there haven't been any animals in there in two decades, the place still smells like hog shit and dry hay. Dust still hangs off every nook and cranny. Cobwebs droop from the rotten boards. Sparrow nests hang from the open rafters. Anyone could break in. They wouldn't even need a sledgehammer—just a will and a strong set of shoulders. Even though I do it in the old well room and chain the doors at night, I know nothing is as secure as I want it to be. But that was a lesson I learned long ago, living in this town. This town of 440. This town that the John Deere factory left. This town that leaves me no other option.

I do it in the barn because I can't stand the smell. It's that ammonia smell. And even though I cook in the barn, I can't escape the smell. *We smell it on you,* Danny Meyer says to me at the Pit Stop. Well, Danny, we can't all be corn farmers, but we can all reap what we sow. I reap powder. White. Keening. Bitter. *You're gonna get yourself killed,* Kay Williams says when I run into her at church. We all die in the end, Kay. But still, I'm careful. Most explosions occur because the cooks are high. I don't use, so I'm not sloppy. *You should be ashamed of yourself,* Bill Putnam says to me at the fire and rescue meetings. *You're a volunteer on this squad; you should have a higher respect for authority—for life.* I'm also a father, Bill. Your approval won't feed my boys; upstanding morals won't buy the gas I need to get them to school.

Today, the wind blows. It whistles through the cracks. The combines are rolling, kicking up corn dust. The loud hum of the wheels as they turn breaks my concentration. I can't do this today. This is how accidents happen. I extinguish the burner, place the chemicals on their shelves. I step out of the old well room, swing the door in place, wrap the chain and padlock around the handle. *Daddy's special alone place,* I tell the boys. *There are monsters in there.*

I step out on the lawn and look to the west. Acres spread before me, rolling on forever. We own the house, the barn, and the three acres they sit on, but we are an island. And we are not the only ones. Danny Meyer bought all the land when farming was bad and spends his days laughing about it at the bar. I look at the land: rows of gold stretching to the blue horizon. I watch the green beasts devour. Leaves take flight. The shaved ground is left with nothing but stubble. A deer lopes out of the way.

My father owned that ground once, sold it when farming was tough—sold it for ten times what my grandfather paid for it. Laughed all the way to the bank. He kept the house and went to work for John Deere, starting a new career legacy for the men in my family. When he died, he left me the house and his regret.

Maybe I was wrong, Danny, I could say. *A lot of the time we reap what others sow.*

I keep looking. The sun glints off the combine's windshield. The cloud of corn dust gets thicker as the machine gets closer. I can barely see. I can barely breathe. It envelopes me. Corn has a smell, too. Dry. Bitter. Keening. The smell of harvest. It's in everything, on all of us. We can't escape what we do. We're all reapers.

The next time I see Danny Meyer, I'll tell him. I'll tell him in the same condescending tone he uses on me. *I can smell it on you, Danny. I can smell it on you, too.*

Poetry – 2nd place
Tim J. Brennan

Self Portrait

The world is round
is what they told him
but he lives near Iowa.
It's not like he'd walk
around the planet
anyway, a dot
on a creased map
wrinkled, each section
threatening to fracture,
folded so many times
creases have creases.

It's a languid stroll
winter, spring, summer,
fall over one bridge
and back again,
all streets rush
themselves off to work,
amble home to a tavern
and tangle back.
A burn in the calf,
a stab in the back,
the lack of breath
in a journey, all
downhill now.

Creative Nonfiction – 2nd place
Charmaine Pappas Donovan

Another Kind of Bonanza

Always on Sundays, after a paltry supper of pancakes or Kraft Macaroni & Cheese, we gathered dirty clothes from hampers, stuffed them into wicker and plastic baskets and drove to the laundromat on Main Street. Mom usually parked in the alley out back where we lugged overflowing containers into the white-walled, gray-floored laundromat smelling of bleach and detergent. Sorting, we dumped Tide into the bottom of each washer, whites and colors placed just so, around each doughnut hole agitator. While the loads moaned monotonously, I shampooed my mother's hair with Prell in a deep commercial sink. Once her wet strands were parted and gelled with Dippity-Do, I twisted Mom's blonde hair onto brush rollers, stabbing white picks into each one to hold it in place. She sat under an industrial hair dryer near the back door reading magazines—*Redbook*, *Good Housekeeping* and *Reader's Digest.* The corners of each worn cover curled at the edges. I listened for the swish of the rinse cycle, the final fluid spin and click as each washer stopped. I wheeled wet clothes in square metal baskets to dryers where for one cent per minute our clothes fluttered dry; buttons scraped the sides of the dryers, whispering silver sounds. I thought about what I was missing on television: *The Ed Sullivan Show* and *Bonanza*. After warm clothes were folded neatly in our baskets, a smile passed between us that was worth every missed minute of television. Mom got rid of her Phyllis Diller rat's nest and I needed that clean gym suit for school the next day.

Fiction – 2nd place
Edis Flowerday

Special Delivery

I drop to the floor of my living room when I see the mail carrier coming. He stalks up the front walk and stuffs my mail into the slot with such force that he rips the cover right off my *New Yorker.* He's a paunchy guy, and his legs are super hairy. I know that because he always wears shorts, even in the winter, which clearly indicates something seriously wrong with his bodily settings. Earbuds are part of his standard equipment. No doubt he's listening to nasty rock that celebrates the joys of rape and murder and mayhem. His big wad of chewing tobacco generates enough juice for him to spit once in front of every house on the block. And he never says a word. Not to anyone. Not even when they smile and say, "Hello. How are you?"

"He'll go postal one of these days," my neighbor George says, as he sits out front of his house, cleaning his shotgun. "He's just the type." George sights down the gun barrel and then blows through it. He picks up the knife he's been using to spear pickled eggs from a jar, and he wipes it on his oil-slicked jeans. Folding the knife and stashing it in his hip pocket, he stands and gives his rear end a little pat. "That guy is unpredictable," he says. "One of these days, he'll explode without warning. Just mark my words, sweetie. We'll read about it in the newspapers. Well, see you around." George disappears into his house. He's a really nice guy, always going hunting with Gus, his big black Labrador. The mail-person has Maced Gus at least twice.

When it comes to things postal, I know I have to face facts and get prepared for impending doom. When that guy runs amok, there'll be a dead body on every front lawn and blood-spattered mail fluttering in the breeze. I can only hope that my neighbor George guns him down before he gets to my house. But I can't rely on that. So I enroll in a self-defense class at the local high school and learn how to kick 'em where it hurts. I also take Tai

Chi for relaxation and confidence and balance; and I install deadbolt locks on the three outside doors of my house. I practice running for help to the neighborhood fire station and find that I can make the trip in less than a minute. I am a little concerned though, that the firefighters always look startled when I come racing up, tag the door with both hands, check my watch, and then go jogging back down the sidewalk. The important thing is that I've stopped freezing up every afternoon just at two when I know I'll hear the lid to the mail slot go *thwang.*

Then come this past Wednesday, someone rings my doorbell three times in rapid succession and starts pounding on the door. It's the postal carrier. I know it. His dander's up about something. But I'm ready. I grab my pepper spray, jerk the door open, and aim right at his face. He looks startled and ducks down, spilling my mail all over the front porch.

"Jeez, lady," he whines, pulling out his earbuds. "All I need is a signature for this package. Will ya' take it easy?"

"I'd love to take it easy," I say. "But, frankly, you don't give me a chance. You deliver the mail like it's a toxic substance. You walk around Macing dogs and cats and canaries. You look mad all the time, like some predatory creep. And that's scary. Not to mention that when people say, 'Hello,' you never answer."

"People talk to me?"

"Yeah. All the time. Haven't you noticed? But do you ever say anything? No, sir. Not you, Mr. Macho Mail-Person."

"Well, I'm listening to my tapes, aren't I?"

"Yeah, like some angry teenager."

He stares at me hard but I don't blink. And then he says "Hey! I'm learning Spanish in twelve easy lessons. You have a problem with that?"

He shoves the signature card in my face. I sign it and hand it back. He tosses the package at my feet. He turns to leave but then he pauses and looks back over his shoulder.

"Hasta la vista, baby," he says. "That's Spanish for 'I'll be back.'"

9

Poetry
Ruth Schmidt-Baeumler

Big Red

I speak another language with him,
enjoy the view above traffic, listen
to CDs while the air conditioner caresses.
I clear away tar marks with butter,
clean out crusted coffee cups,
shake sawdust-filled rugs.

Others RAM him through the woods.
Blown-down trees get hauled out
with a chain attached to Big Red
who somehow endures collisions
with hidden tree stumps, deep soil ruts,
and hanging cedar boughs all of which
gouge out lights, scratch the red paint job,
and delete rearview mirrors.

He comes back to me, patiently awaiting
my supplications. My mewing over carelessness
due to testosterone-powered driving
calms his shaken axle nuts.

Poetry
Marilyn D. Wolff

Spectator Sport

The old white Chevy pickup truck
was parked in the edge of the field,
the field he had turned over
every spring for the last fifty-two years.

The old farmer—dressed in his Red Wing boots,
OshKosh overalls, red flannel shirt,
and John Deere hat—
still looked the part.

His International Tractor
traded in for a white plastic lawn chair
perched in the grass next to the truck
so he could watch the field event.

Today it was the mowing
and the baling of the hay,
the chore turned over
to the son and the grandson.

He, now being reduced to
the smeller of fresh-cut hay and sweat,
the waver, the encourager,
the spectator.

He looked down at his hands
turned over in his lap,
soft white palms up,
and knew he was no longer
a part of the harvesting,
but soon would be the main event.

Poetry
Laura L. Hansen

How to Build a Fire

When the old birch fell
it didn't land with a thud
but with a soft percussive sound
like the sizzle of a snare drum
struck with a brush, or the sound
of dried leaves underfoot
in the autumn.

When the old birch fell
it broke apart in even lengths
as if ready to be stacked
or to be laid on the fire,
as if all those dark
horizontal lines
that ring the tree,

the paper bark split
and unraveling,
were but perforations,
markers for the woodcutter.
I wonder, at the end of this life,
what markers there will be
to pull my body apart,

how it will be laid on the fire.
Will it be evenly stacked?
Will it flash burn or smolder?
That is what I wonder
as I shuffle through the leaves,
step into the next season,
landing first one foot

and then another
into the snow
of my sixtieth year.

Fiction
M. E. Fuller

Abel March

Abel March celebrated his 75th birthday by drowning in Lake Martin, five miles from home.

Abel's wife Sheila had died three months earlier after years of illness. Abel should have been relieved at her passing. She was free from suffering. He was free from watching her suffer. But he felt nothing.

Abel woke on this birthday morning to the sounds of scolding crows. It was the same damned thing every morning. He wished for a shotgun. He was willing to blow out the bedroom window if that would silence those bastards. He imagined their oily black feathers scattered across the lawn to sink out of sight below the ankle-high grasses. He hadn't mowed all summer.

Abel rose from his bed of dirty sheets, nearly black in places. He hadn't done the laundry either. Since Sheila left, Abel couldn't remember a single thing he had done. He stepped into his worn bed slippers and sighed. He shuffled across the room, through planks of early morning sunlight laid out in a rigid pattern across the threadbare green carpet. He opened the bedroom window blinds. He opened the window. He cursed the crows.

Abel made his way to the cluttered kitchen, ignoring the stink of decaying garbage. He thought about making coffee, but was distracted by one thing in all the mess. A sympathy card stood straight up and confident in the mail basket next to the telephone. "We're so sorry for your loss," it read. Abel considered the word *loss*. He wondered at the small, small word. He turned back to the bedroom to dress.

He disrobed then re-robed in torn khaki pants, a wrinkled blue work shirt he retrieved by some effort from the floor, and a pair of leather, ill-fitting sandals. He left the bedroom, the house, and walked with deliberate intention into the garage where he pulled his favorite fishing hat down from its wooden dowel perch.

Outside, Abel climbed into the cab of his sixteen-year old Ram truck with his Crestliner in tow. With one more barrage of curses at the crows to his back, he clicked the automatic door opener and drove off into the sunrise. As the garage door made its slow descent, any passerby could catch a glimpse of a well-used steel tackle box resting on the garage floor in a sliver of disappearing morning light.

Poetry
Darryl Zitzow

Old Timer's Disease

I first met them two years ago.
They were the little people—the Furleys—
only twelve inches tall and they had magic.
It was July and they had turned my furnace up so high,
it was unbearably hot.
And they always seemed to leave my stove burners on
when I left my house.
They made an awful mess, one time,
when they left the water running in my bathtub.
They would even make me forget
how to get home.
They could turn my milk sour
and grow mold in my fridge.
Sometimes they would make
my food in the pantry disappear.
They could make me forget
what I had for breakfast
or whether I even ate dinner at all.
I often saw them playfully run past me,
out of the corner of my eye.
They were full of mischief
but they would never ever hurt me.
My children, when they came to visit,
always complained of the scattered messes they made.
Now my children are afraid for me
and that is why I have to leave my home.
My children don't understand.
I hate to leave.
The Furleys are my friends
and keep me from feeling alone
and I don't know how they'll manage
without me.

Poetry
Mary Lou Brandvik

Whenever

Whenever I smell honeysuckle or sickbeds,

> it is North Dakota in August,
> and I am on the front porch
> rocking in Grandpa's black leather chair,
> reading *Huckleberry Finn*, and
> eating chocolate chip cookies.

> The wheat trucks rumble past, and whirling
> dust filters through the windows.

But this is not my story.

> My story is grandparents in hospital beds
> in the living room,
> dying,
> summer after summer,
> while I read and rock and wish
> myself
>   away.

Creative Nonfiction – Honorable Mention
Norma Thorstad Knapp

How Much She had Lost

Noisy purging sounds greeted me as I stepped into Mom's sparse room. Seconds later, the oxygen concentrator emitted a *tttssshh* sound. Like a straw-slender elephant trunk, tubing hung from Mom's nose. A dark graying pixie haircut haloed her face. A faded yellow robe hung on her frail body, outlining pendulous breasts and a round belly.

A single mother of eight, she'd lost much this past year: a daughter, her home, her health, her independence. Resenting being in a nursing home, she'd tried teaching herself not to care.

"Hi, Mom!" Hearing my voice, she whirled her wheelchair around, energy teeming behind sage eyes. Her chin, like a chicken's clean breastbone, tilted upwards. She visibly softened.

Every month I drove seven hours to be with her. Tomorrow she would celebrate her 85th birthday. A bookkeeper most of her life, she now could not balance her own checkbook. Could not stand alone. Could not walk alone. Could not breathe without help.

We visited about my brothers, her grandchildren, my drive. Later I styled her hair and drove us to Wendy's for a cheeseburger and Frosty—her favorites. We ate in the car. My Asian salad was hot and spicy in my mouth. A mild summer breeze bothered the treetops; cottonwood leaves nuzzled each other. Mom moved the straw around in her paper cup. In the distance, traffic noises blared.

"What would you like for your birthday, Mom?"

She never hesitated. "I'd like to waltz one more time."

Not going to happen, Mom, I thought, remembering how all her life she'd loved to dance. She'd kicked up her heels into her seventies.

That evening, I pondered her request. Earlier I'd organized food, baked a cake, invited family and friends, decorated the Sun Room near her room.

The next day Mom arrived in the Sun Room in her wheelchair, wearing a pursed smile and a lacey beige dress. Smells of coffee and body odors comingled throughout the boisterous room.

She stopped to hug each son and sibling, greet guests, speak to and touch each child's face. Then she wheeled to the head table and dawdled over cake. Later while opening cards and gifts, she thanked each giver, holding her careful self-possession in spaniel-like gratitude.

At length I pushed "Play" on the CD player I'd borrowed. As the room noises receded, Patti Page's raspy voice filled the air.

I was dancing with my darling
to the Tennessee Waltz . . .

I approached Mom, lowered myself, framed her face with my hands, breathed in her perfumy scent, touched my forehead to hers.

"Mommy?" My voice broke. "May I have this dance?"

Nodding, her watery eyes glistened, her mouth a wide smile stretched across her face.

I reached down, swept her to me, helped her stand. She wobbled, tilted back precariously like a sideswiped bowling pin, and sucked the bracing air into her lungs. I held her tightly, her body soft as bread dough.

Like wheat in the wind, we swayed.

Poetry
Kit Rohrbach

Valley Forge
It doesn't matter
where I scatter
the ashes or how they fall from my hand
to land
on leaf or dogwood flower.
One shower,
one storm, and no trace
will remain in this monumental place
where a tattered army camped a deadly winter,
fought to leave a parent
nation, errant
battles for Independence Day
and DNA
disconnected and unraveled.
I have traveled
miles and maybe years,
but there is nothing of you here.
No quick dry wit
no bit
of broader humor
no concession to cancer
no answer
to 6 Across.
Just
dust
which doesn't matter.

Poetry
Frances Ann Crowley

Sunday Morning at the Lake

The sun swaggers up from another zone and begs
dawn to play more jazzy blues.
The horizon draws a tangerine pashmina
around her shoulders.

The town sleeps and dreams of a lake freckled
with boats surfing on sunbeams
and weekenders who litter the beach
with tattoos and tans.

We, who have been betrayed by body and brain,
sit on the porch and gather snapshots from a box—
memorials at once bitter and delicious,
like coffee and newspapers.

Fiction - Honorable Mention
Paisley Kauffmann

The Odds

Things had gone well, almost perfect. They, with guilty pleasure, behind closed doors, admitted they were happy. Responsible living, good decision-making, and hard work had resulted in robust college funds and retirement accounts. They had satisfying careers, interesting hobbies, close friends, and a rescue dog. However, here he is pushing two crumpled dollars across the sticky counter. "One Powerball, please."

The clerk, eyes stitched to his phone, asks, "Picking your own numbers or you want the machine to do it?"

"I'll pick my numbers."

The clerk stuffs his phone into his pocket and the bills into the register. He runs his fingers through his greasy hair and taps the screen of the digital lottery machine. Celestially, it glows to life. The clerk hovers his hand over the integers, and says, "Shoot."

He closes his eyes, inhales through his nose, and is repulsed by the smell of fried chicken and hot dogs. The winning lottery numbers float through the mire to the surface.

"Twenty-four." In a blur of complex medication regimens and frequent vomiting, he and his wife had celebrated twenty-four years of marriage. The scent of two dozen roses wafted through the house triggering her nausea. Holding back her hair, he recalled the first time he saw her striding, head high and shoulders back, across their college campus before she slipped on a patch of ice. He raced to help gather her books and find her glasses. She tucked her loose brown locks behind her ears and frowned at the scratched lens. Even with her furrowed brow and pinched mouth, he thought she was lovely. He gripped her mittened hands, pulled her to her feet, and never let go.

"Okay," the clerk says.

He opens his eyes, and says, "Sorry. Sixty." According to the prognosis, she has sixty days to live. The doctor, rubbing his temples, had informed them of the menacing itinerant mass and granted her six months. Within four months, they accrued a debt of sixty thousand dollars in the high cost of hope. She had always been athletic and vibrant, healthy as a horse. A quotidian ritual, rain or shine, she and the rescue dog jogged five miles before breakfast, while he repeatedly hit snooze. If anyone could beat the egregiously unfavorable odds, she could.

The clerk raises his eyebrows.

"Three." She had endured three rounds of chemotherapy and radiation. The exasperated oncologist had reiterated the intention of chemo-radiation was exclusively for pain management. After each treatment, between bouts of heaving, she apologized for her diagnosis, abandoning him, and the financial burden. She cursed herself for leaving the kids He had pressed his palms to his ears and shouted at her—swore at her—to shut up. In stunned alarm, she widened her owl-like eyes, large in her bald head, and stopped. That moment is one of his many regrets.

"Twenty-one." Twenty-one years ago, their son was born. After three years of charting her basal temperature and cervical mucus, they repressed tears of joy until she burst from the bathroom waving the positive pregnancy test. Although difficult to conceive, he was an easy and contented baby with his father's bright blue eyes and his mother's natural optimism. Their golden-haired child believes his mother will prevail and live to see him graduate college in the spring. No one has the heart to tell him otherwise.

A man waiting to pay for his beef burrito and doughnut

scratches his beard and sighs.

The clerk urges him to continue. "And?"

"Fourteen." The age of their surprise child: the unexpected and tempestuous daughter. An effortless, yet conflicted pregnancy provoking tears of frustration after returning to the work force and landing her first corporate account. The relentless morning sickness and fatigue brought her to her knees and to the emergency room for rehydration. After a string of sleepless nights with their screaming newborn, they humorously decided there was an inverse relationship between the ease of conception and the temperament of the baby. Their daughter refuses to accept the diagnosis and rages against the absence of her mother from her future graduation, wedding, and motherhood. He has secretly and regretfully poached her college fund for the experimental, animal-tested treatments. His daughter's scowl tells him what he already knows; he should be the one fading away, not her mother.

"And your Powerball number?" the clerk asks, glancing at the line of customers.

His biggest fear, his worst nightmare, is to be alone. "One."

Poetry
Sharon Harris

Genevieve Irene Ferrier Story (Jennie)
1893-1921

I'm sorry

when I went to sleep
last night
very ill and weak
I fully believed
I would greet the dawn
and be stronger

I'd rise early
to start the day
to fix your breakfast
and to work beside your father
in the barn
or in the field

I fully believed
I'd be up with the dawn
and be there
to kiss you awake

I'm sorry
my three little ones
I didn't mean
to leave you

Fiction
Cindy Fox

Memory Lapse

On this January morning, the coffee pot sputters and hisses when I sneak a cup before it's done. I pinch the cream container's mouth that won't push open where it says it should. I pry apart its sealed lips with a butter knife, splashing a hefty dose of cream into my coffee cup as more drools down its chin. I wipe the puddle from the counter with the last paper towel, clutching it in my hand, lest I forget to add "paper towels" to my grocery list.

The newspaper's "Savvy Senior" column touts repetition is the key for memory retention. I take this advice seriously and type my user name and password in my email account each day. Besides, I wouldn't know where I hid my list with my secret identity should Yahoo! ask, "Forgot your password?" Then they'd ask dumb questions like, "What city was your mother born in?" How the hell do I know? Why don't they ask me something I know?

Before logging out I delete my spam messages, like taking out the garbage, then sit at the kitchen table to review my to-do list: dust, pick up RX, groceries. The vacuum cleaner stands next to the living room wall and I remember vacuuming yesterday. I add "vacuum" to the list and then cross it off. But why isn't she in the closet? She has something else to do, but she stares back at me, her cord tangled on the floor like untied apron strings.

I rank my list in order of importance. My prescription is ready for pick-up, so I move my trip to the drugstore to the top. I pull on black polyester slacks with a stretchy waistband and frown at the pant legs pooling on the floor. Hitching them up, I berate myself for not adding "hemming" to my list the day I bought them. I poke my head through my favorite sweatshirt, admiring the embroidered cardinal perched on my left breast, and grope for the armholes like a bird with broken wings.

I check my purse for keys three times before walking out the door. I retrace my steps and snatch my grocery list that peeks from under a paper towel on the table. Checking the list for missing items, I remember the other day while whipping up a cake, batter splattered all over the place; my hands were too sticky to add whatever it was I needed to my grocery list. So, like a vigilante, I rummage through canisters and pantry shelves for that missing staple. I find flour, sugar, vanilla, butter, but don't see the missing egg carton in the refrigerator.

The pharmacy is a sea of my lady friends' bobbing white heads. We exchange hellos along with our ailments while waiting in line for our prescriptions: pills to lubricate joints, pills to stop leaks, pills to unplug clogged arteries, pills to keep bones from breaking when bifocal lines cause a misstep.

Approaching the supermarket, the parking lot is a jumble of granny cars that look like they ran out of gas before easing into their parking spots. I pride my forethought to shop for groceries today—the only day of the week seniors receive a 5% discount. Up and down the aisles, my shopping cart wobbles as if it has a broken ankle while my pant legs sweep the floor. I buy cream in a plastic bottle, but don't see eggs nestled in their cartons. I cross "toilet tissue" off my list and admire the man with the brawny shoulders as I rumble past the paper towels to the checkout counter.

Back home, my husband ransacks each bag. "Where are the vacuum cleaner bags?" he asks. "Yesterday you asked me to change the bag, but we were out. Didn't you add them to your list?"

"I forgot."

Head slumped, I swallow a sob as my new pants weep a brown, watery substance onto the kitchen floor. I reach for a paper towel and the naked cardboard roll pushes me over the edge. I turn to look at Mrs. Hoover who waits for her diaper to be changed. I shove her in the closet and kick the door shut.

I need a friend's shoulder to cry on, like a Facebook friend who will comment with a smiley face. I press the Start button on my computer a little harder than necessary. I stare at the log-in screen. My head pulses as the cursor blinks and waits.

Poetry
Alberta Lee Orcutt

After a Hard Day's Work

Big fingers
 sinewy
 from pulling teats
 and pushing the plow

 peppered
 with scrubbed
 ground-in dirt

pull the dainty thread
through the taut cloth.

The hoop is held close to his overall bib,
the white forehead across a red face
furrowed in concentration.

So engrossed is he in his
dishtowel embroidery—
lazy-daisy petal stitches—

he does not look up
when the TV announces
a rise in corn prices.

It is the habit of daisies
to close their petals
when the sun goes down.

Outside the window
white rays fold over
golden disks

taking quiet notice
of a steady worker,
letting him be.

Poetry
Susan Niemela Vollmer

Peace

The unfinished burdens hang over us
But this is briefly our place to rest

Next to the quiet water
Where the trees mirror themselves

With sunlight on our backs
And shadows gathered beside us

Fiction
Cheyenne Marco

Baptismal

Leda sat on the couch, a glass of bourbon in one hand and her family photo album in the other. She heard the crack of concrete splitting, and she felt the thunder of water rushing across the land. Her cause of death wouldn't be that she hadn't known it was coming. She had known since the rain had begun to fall that the dam wouldn't hold. The radio had been broadcasting it for hours. Piercing sirens called out in alarm.

There were some walls that weren't meant to hold. Some structures were just bound to break.

In the photo album, she had collected images of a life, the kind she mused her son might have lived. But Sam was gone, in a world she could only reach through water.

She flipped through the still-lifes. The first photo was one of her in a dress she only remembered as white. Now, the aged frame suggested something closer to egg shell and she knew that, buried deep in the attic, the dress was probably closer to yellow—if it even existed at all anymore. Anton stood by her side, wiry and lean as ever. His arms and legs looked like noodles, and she remembered her mother's words about Anton not being a man of strength.

There were few pictures between the ones of her wedding and the one of her blooming with a bump of life, distending her belly and burning her soul. Even through the lens of time and the grainy image, she knew that the child protected by her skin and the film of the photo did not have wiry limbs, did not have Anton's sharp nose. There had never been enough layers to bury that truth, not enough water to wash that sin away.

She knew Anton knew. The way he looked at her in the next frames immortalized that suspicion. His hands never hovered near her belly. Fatherly love didn't flow from the page. Still, he held the baby, cradled him in arms made strong by the Army Corp of Engineers. He built bridges and dams, avoided building them in their lives. When he didn't come home one day, when a cop and a

29

man in a suit came to the door, she found herself wondering what the story would be. It would be an accident for sure, but she would never stop wondering how much was truth, how much an architect he had been in his own demise. He had wanted to die. This she knew. That had been his truth. Long before the baby. It had driven her to the arms of another man: a temporary respite in life.

The baby cried long into the nights right after Anton's death. She pretended he missed his father. She ignored the fever and the rash, using Anton's death to soothe it away. The baby was hot with his passion. The baby was red with his indignation. His belly swelled with the grief he felt for his father. When the baby's last breath gurgled into silence, Leda thanked God. She felt a release. Maybe it could all be better now.

Leda closed her album and nestled it in her lap. She gulped down what was left in the glass and set it on her end table. She gripped the book tighter. It was her last resolve. When the waters would come, she would not let go. She would carry it with her into the afterworld. What she hadn't been able to hold onto then, she would hold onto now. This would be her almighty test.

She felt the water draw closer. It sounded like hooves galloping toward her. Her heart started to beat with the imaginary herd. It pitched to a deafening roar, and she hugged her entire body around her album. *Never let go. Never let go.* She wanted to squeeze her eyes shut, but she needed to watch, needed to see God destroy what was left. Walls burst from the seams. The furniture tumbled. Everything flew forward from force.

A wind, first, embraced her, giving her a hint of the cold. She didn't have long to process it before the water slapped into her body. The breath went out of her, knocking her over and around like a rag doll. Her body twirled and turned and churned. All she could see was darkness. As her lungs burned for air, her empty arms stretched out; she floated in nothingness, thinking only *Never let go.*

Fiction
Chet Corey

Dependents

"Look around for my gloves," she said.

He felt between the café booth's cushions until he found one glove and then the other. He wondered what might be found beneath cushions of the old davenport, as in childhood he had found the nickels, quarters and dimes he'd secretly kept.

As much as he was able, hesitatingly he asked, "When Dad was alive, did Dad take two dependents or one?"

When she didn't answer, he asked if she claimed herself on Social Security, explaining how he claimed no dependents and got more of a tax return.

"I don't have dependents," she said.

"You have yourself," he said, "and are entitled to either one or none."

"How far did we park?" she asked.

He let it go for a better time and, from behind her, held out her winter coat and waited for her to sort out her arms—for her to follow frayed lining until each hand felt its worn cuff.

"I forgot to bring my cane," she said, taking his arm.

But whose arm was this, she wondered. *Her father's? Were they walking down St. Ansgar's narrow aisle?* Everyone in the pews was turning toward her, but she'd keep her veiled eyes straight ahead. Steady and straight ahead.

"It isn't far," he said, suddenly seized by the strength of his mother's grip.

Fiction
Dan McKay

Lufthansa Flight 401

The room was cold, just like always. No gown this time, only test results. The doctor, freshly tanned, wore a Hawaiian shirt under his lab coat. "My wife and I just got back from a cruise. I don't know why we didn't do it years ago. Do you have a dream vacation, one where you just drop everything and go?"

"I've always wanted to fly to Italy. See where Grandpa was born."

The doctor nodded. "I'd book it soon."

Poetry
Kristin Laurel

Small Prayer

I know a poet who takes her best work
and buries it in her backyard.
She calls them her prayers.

My sister has buried both of her children.
I cannot bury these poems.
I am still trying to pray.

Poetry
Alberta Lee Orcutt

Self-Compassion

She dragged the wooden lawn chair, splintered, paint chipped—
just like me, she thought with a chuckle as she coaxed it to the
dappled shade of the lilac bush. She eased herself into it, adjusted
herself in favor of the sore hip, leaned back, crossed her feet at
the ankles, rested her arms across her stomach, and closed her
eyes.

The breeze baptized her in sweet lilac fragrance: her straw hair,
her flowered cutoffs, faded gingham shirt, gnarled toes. She
basked in the perfume. Yes, there were house chores to be done,
flower beds to be tilled with a bent dinner fork. They'd be there
tomorrow.

She dozed, dreamed of the aroma of her dad's fried apple pies, her
mom's wild plum jam and hot buttered biscuits.

After a full hour of bliss, she roused herself, stood, and, with a
yawn, stretched her arms to the sky. Then, she curtsied to the
lilac bush. Sore hip and all.

Poetry
David Eric Northington

Nursing Homes
It's like a movie sequel
Or a car accident
That happens over and over
Two parents in a nursing home
Separated by twelve years
And a slow painful death for her
The final scene is approaching
A different actor, Oscar-winning performance
The final curtain call

Fiction
Charles Johnson

Bracelets

Gone! Her precious homecoming bracelet! With a panicked hoot, Sharon stood in alarm and dashed from the kitchen to her bedroom.

She rummaged through her jewelry box. Nothing. She flung the box to the floor, breaking the lid in two. She yanked out dresser drawers, contents falling in heaps. The bed stand? Empty. Sharon toppled it in frustration, the lamp falling and shattering. She checked boxes in her closet. She stood in the disheveled room, wondering, *Where now?*

She needed her bracelet for the day's homecoming events. She was a queen candidate; the bracelet was her lucky charm. A gift from her boyfriend Ron, it was a slender, silver chain with a matching plate, "SHARON AND RON" engraved on front, "1964" on back.

Sharon raced from room to room, finding no sign of her cherished bracelet. Tears welled in her eyes. She simply must find it.

Ah, yes! Her best friend Krissy lived just down the road. Perhaps she had left the bracelet there. Sharon bolted out into the mid-morning sun, bound for Krissy's. She weaved through trees, ducking branches, swinging some out of the way. It was farther than she remembered.

At Krissy's, she let herself in. "Anyone home?" No answer. Sharon headed to Krissy's room.

Sharon parked herself at Krissy's vanity. Lipsticks, compacts and barrettes flew as she dug through the drawers. Finding nothing, she angrily slammed her hand on the vanity, catching her reflection in the mirror. Her face looked so plain. That wouldn't do. She eyed Krissy's makeup on the vanity. Strawberry reds and bright yellows: Krissy's favorites.

Did she hear her name called? She listened closely. She listened again: nothing. She began to do her makeup.

Despite her anxiety, Sharon skillfully applied blush, mascara and eyeliner. Ron would like how she looked—but she genuinely needed that bracelet.

Krissy's jewelry box sat on the dresser. Sharon inspected each section. Zilch. As she turned to leave, her eyes caught a glint from the bed stand. No bracelet, but next to the radio lay tan earrings with gold trim that she had lent Krissy. Pocketing them, she wondered, *Where? Where?*

Again! Had someone called to her? The voice seemed remote, so she ignored it.

Krissy kept her personal keepsakes under the bed! She knelt on a strangely damp and mushy carpet, raising the bedspread to let in light. She crawled into the dimness; no sign of Krissy's special stash. With an unladylike curse, she rapidly backed out, gashing her knee as she emerged. Grimacing, she stood too quickly and fainted, hitting her head as she fell.

***

The doctor met Ron at the exam room door just before midnight.

"What's the word, Doc? How's my wife?"

"Policeman brought her in fifteen minutes ago—cuts on her knees, pollen and berry juice on her face, a bump on her forehead and she had a few acorns in her pocket. She'll be okay. How long had she been missing?"

"Fourteen frightening hours. It's the first time she's taken off. They found her in the woods east of town? "

"Correct. You'll want to contact her doctor and get her meds assessed. How old is she?"

"Seventy-four. We've been married fifty-three years now."

"She'll be fine in time. I'll be just down the hall." He opened the door for Ron and left.

Entering the room, Ron found Sharon dozing on a bed, breathing softly.

She stirred. Recognition crossed her face and settled clearly in her eyes. "Oh . . . a hospital?" She spotted her husband. "Why am I here, Ron?"

A nurse finished bandaging Sharon's knee and nodded to Ron as she left. She told him she'd be right back.

"What happened, Ron?" The short rest had opened a level of alertness in her face that Ron hadn't seen in months.

Ron sat on the bed, helping her sit up. "You wandered off today, Sharon."

"I'm sorry, Ron. I get so confused. Are you mad?"

He reassured her with a hug. "Not at all. I'm just glad they found you. We'll get you home tonight."

Sharon nodded with a tired, flickering motion as the awareness that had dawned in her eyes evaporated. She noticed the hospital arm band on her wrist and smiled that blank smile that Ron had seen on her face for so many mornings. She lifted her arm for him to see.

"Look! I found my homecoming bracelet."

Creative Nonfiction
Virginia Eckert

the bed on the couch

I lay in my bed, cocooned in my covers, overcome by chills and dripping with sweat. The high fever brings me back to my childhood. My twenty-seven-year-old body disappears and I am now six or seven or eight. Lying down on the bed that my mother made for me on the couch. Carefully propped up by just the right amount of pillows. She left the blanket open so that I could crawl in, and then draped it over me, tucking me in tight. There is a cool, wet washcloth that she carefully folded and placed across my forehead. A plateful of saltine crackers that she set on the table in front of me. Next to the clamshell Lion King VHS case. I have memories of her approaching me with a small glass of Sprite and a spoon, feeding me the liquid, spoonful by spoonful. And occasionally rubbing Vicks VapoRub on my chest. But now I am burning up and unable to sleep. I don't have the crackers. Or the spoonfuls of Sprite. And I don't even have a VCR. And I wish I was there, safe, in the bed on the couch that my mom made.

Creative Nonfiction
Tarah L. Wolff

Lake Rocks

The first five years of my life were spent on East Crooked in Minnesota, the deepest, rockiest lake I've ever known. It wasn't green with algae or rank with that sweet of seaweed or fish. It smelled like winter and it was cold all of the time. A lot of people have died in East Crooked and that was something I understood even at five years old. It was perilous without ever having to yell or belittle. It did not have to laugh at you to feel bigger then you.

It was my father who took me from East Crooked.

This is about the things we don't tell people. The things we hold in our mouths like marbles and swallow them down like secrets we want to keep. We try to forget them but instead we go to them anyway, and often, like tongues seeking the jagged edge of a cracked molar. We don't know it until our tongues bleed. And we do bleed. We hemorrhage until one day we look in the mirror and the secrets have changed our faces, left the kids we were behind.

I know now those weren't marbles I was swallowing though; they were lake rocks, run smooth by cold, dark water. And, even as I was being driven away, she ran down to the shore in her little black and pink polka dot swimming suit, where she slipped in and East Crooked kept her.

My husband went fishing there not long ago and I almost asked him if he caught a glimpse of the little girl I used to be.

Poetry
Elizabeth Weir

Our Span in Time

A six-branched snowflake
glances onto my black glove.

Fine filaments of ice
criss-cross in fine perfection.

My close regard
blunts its crystal design.

The flake puckers into itself
and, in a breath, is gone.

Creative Nonfiction
Katie Gilbertson

Halloween

1959. Second grade, age six. On Halloween, the school kids dressed up and marched through the classrooms. I didn't want any cheap costume and dumb mask so no one knew who I was. I wanted a costume like the girls whose mothers sewed. I decided to make my own costume. I would be a French painter! Where I got the idea, I don't know but apparently it made quite an impression on me.

This lofty goal required a paint pallet and brush, obtained secretly from my sister's art set. I needed an over-sized shirt from my dad, red tights and a beret. The beret would send the costume over the top and I would surely win a medal!

My mother wouldn't buy me a beret to wear for one day. On October 30, I was brokenhearted since the beret was key to the outfit. I knew better than to cry in front of my parents as they were firmly opposed to whining, but my muffled sobs into my chenille bedspread apparently moved Mom somehow.

My mother could sew up rips, but I had never seen her do anything else. But she was resourceful so she took a pair of new red underwear and sacrificed them to the cause.

After I went to bed, she got some red thread, sewed up the legs, then gathered them together. She made a pompom of red yarn and sewed it on top. Instant beret!

Halloween morning the beret was sitting on the breakfast table. I was overcome! The elastic waistband fit perfectly around my large six-year-old head. I was able to drape the fabric jauntily for the perfect beret effect. I gave my mother a hug and took my costume to school.

After lunch, giddy with excitement, I put on my costume. I

carefully arranged the beret, pleased that the color perfectly matched my red tights.

Brandishing my stolen art pallet and brush, I was ready to parade around in all my glory. My teacher looked at me a little oddly and two kids stared at my head in amazement. I was ecstatic!

That parade was the pinnacle of my life. Kids pointed. The word spread. The music teacher and speech therapist came out for a look. I hammed it up. I brandished my pallet. I mimed painting in the air. I pranced and posed, causing a commotion. Truly the best day of my life!

Back in my classroom, everyone was smiling and laughing. Then a little girl who had recently moved to the States from England, said, "Hello, Knicker Noggin."

The teacher struggled to restore order. All the kids chanted my new nickname which I bore till middle school.

On the way home I threw the beret in the street and watched a car run over it.

Creative Nonfiction
Louise Bottrell

A Few Good Things

Our son Mike was a shy little boy. He preferred to play in our home with his best friend Tim and occasionally a couple of other boys from the neighborhood. Making new friends and facing new situations were not easy for him.

In junior high, Mike played football and gained acceptance from his role on the team. Andy, the coach, awarded a skull-and-crossbones sticker for the helmet of a player who did something outstanding in a game. These were hard to come by, but Andy made sure each boy received at least one during the season. Mike gained confidence that year and enjoyed his friends.

At the end of the football season, I thanked Andy. Over the years, I silently continued to thank him, often telling new friends the story of how Andy's encouragement and Mike's success as a football player in junior high had made such a difference.

Twenty-five years later Mike and I were having one of our late-night debates, and the conversation turned to confidence. I mentioned how much I had appreciated Coach Andy's helping Mike overcome his shyness.

Mike looked surprised. "Mom, it wasn't Andy. It was that book you gave me to read."

"What book?"

"Don't you remember that book on shyness you gave me? I read it, saw myself, and followed the advice. It worked."

I did vaguely remember ordering a book on overcoming shyness. I had read the book, told Mike he could read it if he liked, laid it on his bed, and forgotten it.

What a gift to learn the book I had given my son in 1973 had played a positive part in his development.

Now as I hurtle toward age seventy-five, I sometimes lie awake at night reliving mistakes, regretting things I cannot change, second-guessing parenting decisions made years ago, thinking of friends and loved ones I let down. Then I remind myself of the shyness book. Perhaps I have accomplished a few good things I do not even know about yet. Perhaps I never will know about them. I close my eyes and fall asleep.

Poetry
Susan Niemela Vollmer

The Memory of Pain

After the pull and twist has subsided
The image remains
Like that of the snake that slithered
Underfoot across the path
No longer visible
But anticipated
In every leaf's quake and tremble

Poetry
Kevin Zepper

Skins

While the big people mingle, we play with the coats, hiding under denim, leather, and goose down. We pull out the card table and arrange the skins on top to form a yurt. The carpet turns to tundra yet we are safe and warm inside the hut. We take out the flashlight we snuck from the junk drawer and hold it under our chins, our sockets hollowing and inky shadows drawing long along our jaw lines. Our teeth shine white and yellow as we laugh in the rapidly growing warmth of the shelter. We place our hands over the bright lenses and see our finger bones through glowing orange flesh. Then, with the light out, we tell stories, like the one about the boy who ran away and was raised by wolves in the northwoods. Or the girl who found out she was adopted, her real parents in a country across the ocean. I open the flap of animal skin and let the cool air renew ours. Soon, we lose a piece of roof, then part of a wall. Our fort slowly erodes as the grown-ups leave, cannibalizing our patchwork world.

Poetry
Audrey Kletscher Helbling

Not Quite Perfect Penmanship

Seated at a desk near the blackboard,
I sweep letters across paper
as Mrs. Pedersen preaches
perfect practiced penmanship.
Properly cross *t*'s. Dot *i*'s. Snake your *s*.
Space lowercase print *l*'s
in straight power pole line precision.

I obey, pressing pencil point upon paper
to draw bare branches of a cottonwood,
rungs of a haymow ladder,
the curving backs of Holstein cows.
Mrs. Pedersen examines my lines of *y*'s, *h*'s, *n*'s,
then thumbs a foil silver star next to my name,
scrawled in subtle rebellion against her rigid rules.

Creative Nonfiction
Beverly Abear

Dark Corridor

The squawks and screeches of our plastic flute-like Tonettes have ceased while Teacher's voice drones on in the warm classroom, crowded with fourth graders. Odors of leftover contents of sack lunches, chalk dust, and sweat make me wish she would open a window or two.

I sit quietly in my desk and try to listen, longing to go out into the cool dark hallway. Maybe I will ask to go to the lav and escape for a few minutes. I lean on my Tonette and sigh. The mouthpiece picks up my errant breath with a shrill bleat and thirty kids stare at me.

Teacher demands, "Who did that?"

Shrinking into my seat, I raise my hand.

Her eyes wide with disbelief at misbehavior from this unexpected quarter, Teacher orders me to stand in the hall, but does not sound angry.

The hall smells of floor cleaner. I am mortified as I stand in the same dark corridor I longed for as an escape but now must endure as punishment. A girl passes. I pretend I'm walking to the lav, pausing to pull up my anklets so she won't guess the truth. Moments pass. Footsteps echo down the hall as the principal approaches. He gives me a nod. I manage a smile.

Fear and anger knot my stomach. It's so unfair. I didn't mean to do it. I just leaned on the stupid thing and breathed. Who knew just *breathing* could get you in trouble?

Tears threaten my nine-year-old eyes that have barely seen sadness or tragedy until this year.

Slumped against the wall, I remember last fall when Teacher announced the President had been shot. Her voice sounded choked. Fear showed on all our faces. His death still seems impossible. Horrible.

I remember earlier this spring when our babysitter's daughter died of double pneumonia. We tried suffocating ourselves with plastic bags so we could be with her in heaven.

I shudder as I remember yesterday when I hurried to answer the incessant ring of our kitchen phone but found Dad already speaking softly into the receiver. He saw me and his angry glare sent me scurrying back to my room, hurt and confused. That's when I knew Mom's accusations of his flirting must be true and he was talking to some woman. I sat on the bed, my arms hugging my knees, and thought of the D word Mom had forbidden us to use. I wondered if someday Divorce would break out family apart.

In a few months' time, I've learned that sometimes life isn't fair at all. People in the world can be violent. Innocent babies die. Fathers betray even the best of mothers. Families break and hearts break and the fear and regret follow us a long time.

And I get sent out of the room for breathing.

My classroom door creaks open and a classmate beckons me inside. Relieved, I step back into the sunlit room.

Poetry
Karla Klinger

Mother/Child

Well past bedtime,
little sister
        (from a warren of warmth
        beneath her quilts)
giggles, whispers to her sister
across the bedroom cold.

Sshh! Mother will hear us,
we caution each other
but the night's conspiracy proceeds.

Mother's steps,
emphatically approaching,
stop outside the door:
It's past your bedtime, girls.
Don't make me speak to you again.
Is she angry? we wonder.

Now those mother's steps are mine,
as my son laughs with his friend
well past a sensible hour.

As I approach the boys
to tell them to settle down
the sister I was at six
        walks with me
        and, abruptly,
I am both mother and child.

Fiction
Tarah L. Wolff

Senior year

We each had our first car. (Rusty old beaters that groaned every time we started them.) It was a cold, snow-forsaken winter, glassing the lakes over with several feet of clear ice. We took them out there (some buddies and us) sharing peppermint schnapps, passing it from car to car. We howled out our favorite songs like dogs with our windows down. We learned to slide and glide, how to turn to regain control, how to bank, how to use the wheel, how to listen to our cars through our feet and hands. By the time the sun came up, I could slide my car sideways twenty feet and stop with inches to spare. Our high school boyfriends saluted us with their bottles held high. When we drove off that lake we knew we could take those cars anywhere and never lose control.

We felt certain and brave.

That was the last time I ever felt like that.

Creative Nonfiction
Cheyenne Marco

Fossils

Staring out the car window, watching grass roll out of ditches and onto mountains that block out the sky, my boyfriend David tells me the myth of Mount Timpanogos. I look to the peaks—jagged and snow-topped. He says a princess sacrificed herself to the gods; they made the mountain out of her sleeping form. I look at the silhouette and trace the sloping nose, the scoop of the neck, the slouched bosom. I think how she will rest there for eternity, unless roused by an angry people who no longer believe in her gods, who only worship what they can bleed from the earth. For now, I admire her for what she is: a legend.

"You know what is the saddest thing I know?" I propose, afraid of my own reverie. "That I will never know all the stories."

"Isn't that good?" David asks, staying focused on the road. "Wouldn't it be sadder to run out?"

"Maybe. But I want to know them all."

I yearn to learn the legends of the land, to know the infinite truth that lies beneath my feet. Each blade of grass has a story that goes back to the mass that oozed out of the sea. A speck became a molecule became a gene became a blade of big bluestem. That blade of grass reproduced, again and again. Was trampled on by bison. Camped on by wanderers. It lay dormant. It sprouted. It died. It birthed blades for pioneers, the railroad—for me. It was part of a history I could never experience.

As I contemplate the weedy ditches, I know there are stories I will never know. I will never be able to interview the birds, never learn the secrets of the willows. But it is not the secretive tongue of Mother Nature that leaves me weary. It is the strangling hand that silences her. Another sad thing I know is that there is not enough space. We build homes, plant more fields, generate more waste. It all goes somewhere. Buried in mountains. Ripped out of grasslands. More than anything, *these* are the stories that go untold. No one notices. I watch the politics. No one cares. These stories go untold for other reasons. Political reasons. Classified reasons. Unreasonable reasons. But the end result is the same: we will never know.

When I jog on the sidewalk running against the Vermillion River—more land robbed of trees and devoted to concrete—I come across the imprint of a leaf in the cement. A little way over, there are the markings of a squirrel's tiny toes. I consider the leaf that rotted away, leaving its image in stone. I wonder what prompted the squirrel to leave a mark of his own. The impressions haunt me. Fossils. Remainders of organisms long gone. I wonder if one day this may be all we have left. When the mountains are glowing and the rivers are dry, we'll have legends in concrete. More stories to tell.

Creative Nonfiction
Dianne M. DelGiorno

The Interview

Every first class meeting, the same final activity: an invitation to interview me, their instructor. That day, like so many others, they asked about the past—my background, my schooling, my successes, my failures. They asked about the present—my family, my likes, my dislikes, my dreams. The questions and answers crisscrossed with ease and speed, humor and joy. Then one question departed from the rest.

"The best," a young man began, smiling in his eagerness to ask the unexpected. "What is the best thing you have ever done?"

Pinnacle, unsurpassable moment, life-altering single point of time and experience—he waited to hear. His fellow students leaned forward with him, waiting to hear. Even the walls leaned in, anticipating a singular stunning moment: wedding day, birth of a child, invention, publication, cancer conquered, journey to some mountaintop, real or metaphor.

I gathered my first choices. I discarded them quickly. And into the emptiness came the answer that surprised all of us. "There is no one 'best.'"

"No best?"

"No one best. The best happens often. The best is to do work I love with those I love. Love and work, intertwined. That is 'the best.'"

"Just love and work?"

"Just love and work."

"Like this very moment?"

"Like this very moment."

Poetry
Sue Bruns

Wrong Turn

I took a wrong turn
And ended up in your life.

Lost, now, in a tangled maze of streets,
I wander through this silent neighborhood and
peer into its vacant alleys, looking for an exit.
The heads of lamp posts, useless sentinels, black and cold, shed
                    no light.
Steam clouds rise from sewer grates and hover like muted ghosts,
then disintegrate like vaporized dreams.
In empty doorways, I search for something familiar;
in unlit windows, no reflection comforts me.
The fading echoes of my footsteps on the dreary, rain-streaked
                    sidewalks
are the only trace of my passing.

There is no map, no GPS to tell me
how to get out of your life.

Creative Nonfiction – Honorable Mention
Pagyn Alexander

Canned Cranberries

Standing in the dining room doorway, I heard my mother's not-so-quiet voice say, "Do you see the way she dresses him? And those curls at the back of his neck. Good Lord, the child needs a haircut."

Mom was talking to her sister about my four-year-old son, standing behind me. I pulled him close, let the half-open door shield us, and listened.

"She treats him like a girl," Mom continued. "Whoever heard of a boy having a baby doll? He calls it Baby Billy."

"She's doing the best she can," Aunt Lillian said.

"Well, the best she can isn't good enough. Did you see what she brought? Canned cranberries. Whoever heard of someone bringing canned cranberries? She said she didn't know that cranberries came in a bag or that she was supposed to cook them."

"Cleo, can't you be grateful she came?"

"She's the one who should be grateful. I loaned her money to buy a car and leave that no-good husband of hers. If only her sisters were around. Maybe they could help. At least they would have known not to bring cranberries in a can."

I placed the green bean casserole back on the kitchen counter, knelt beside Jack, and winked as I nodded toward the back door. He grabbed Baby Billy while I slipped my purse and our jackets off their hooks. A minute later, the fresh outdoor air hit our faces.

When I started the car, I got the giggles and laughed all the way to our tiny apartment. We munched on popcorn and played Candy Land all afternoon. A while later, I baked a frozen pizza and served root beer floats for dessert. As I tucked Jack into bed, he turned to Baby Billy and said, "This was the best Turkey Day ever." I kissed his forehead before turning off the light. "Nighty night. Sleep tight," I whispered and caught a tear with the back of my hand so he wouldn't notice.

Poetry
Ronald j. Palmer

Again Eighteen
In mind the Spring
although the soul
knows the toll that
Winter brings.

What joy, what pain—
a young woman's laugh.

Creative Nonfiction
Beth L. Voigt

No one Ever Told Me

When I was pregnant, I was warned about the morning sickness that could attack at any time of day, about grueling labor that was more exhausting than running a marathon, and about the fright and pain of emergency C-sections with long recoveries.

But no one ever told me about the utter surprise at feeling a flutter of kicks from inside my belly. Or weeks later, the thrill at seeing my infant daughter turn towards my voice for the very first time. Or the giddiness at watching my six-month-old laugh so hard she had tears in her eyes.

And yet, each time I held my newborn in my arms, well-wishers told me about the months (or years!) of sleepless nights to come, about the nonstop crying jags that would leave me worn out and irritable, and about the constant change of diapers and frustrating toilet training to follow.

But no one ever told me that my daughter would ask me one day, "Can we go camping in Never Never Land?" Or that she'd query me, "Why do they call it private parts? I only know about one part." Or that she'd ask, "Mom, when I grow up, can I be an adult?"

And as my daughter grew, I heard all about the "terrible twos" that begin at eighteen months and lasted until three years, the endless question "Why?" to every other statement, and the immediate response, "No!" to most requests no matter how pleasantly phrased.

But no one mentioned that my daughter would call sherbet "sher-Bert and Ernie." Or that, during a hailstorm, she'd say, "Hey, Mom, music's playing on our car." Or that she'd ask, "Has Daddy ever seen you naked?"

No one ever told me she'd hand me my pantyhose one morning and say, "Put on your skin, Mom." Or that, after answering the phone, she'd yell excitedly, "Mom, Mom, I took a message," but had no idea who had called or why.

As she grew into adolescence, I was warned of the unpredictable mood swings, volatile arguments over seemingly small issues, and outright defiance as she pushed me away and sought her independence.

But no one ever told me that she would give me one of the most wonderful gifts simply by writing, "I love you, Mom," on a piece of paper and handing it to me as I talked with a co-worker on the telephone.

Fiction
Michael Kiesow Moore

a wolf dreams he is me

It is a strange dream, being inside the skin of a man. It feels like I sit on my haunches watching from inside, seeing the things unfold through his eyes. We go through his day, first sipping a morning coffee—black—then putting clothes on, driving in a car. I know what cars are from the outside. But if I just sit and watch, I can observe my manself do the driving. And then this man spends his day typing at a computer. What a horror of a dream! All these things keep this man from tearing his clothes off and running through the woods. Does he never dream of leaping at a deer and tearing its throat, the blood gushing into his mouth? What is this thing called "tofu," and why does he use implements for its eating? The day ends with this man taking a bath, sitting in hot water, drinking tea. I like being naked again, and the water is strangely soothing. This is not awful. But the worst part of this dream is smelling nothing. It is as if the world in all its rich dimensions went flat and lost its color. I never get used to that. Finally the dream ends and I awake to cold air brushing my fur. I take a whiff. I smell the world.

Poetry
Marlene Mattila Stoehr

Seasons of My Childhood

Willow catkins, shy forerunners of spring,
whisper, "Shed winter underwear."
Buttercups bloom by swampy hummocks,
homemade kites trail ragged tails, and
chicks arrive in the mailman's Chevrolet.

Summer freshness follows rain as a
rainbow hangs drying in the eastern sky.
Barefoot, we splash in pothole puddles,
squishing soft mud between our toes;
at night chase glowing fireflies, by day
grow rich picking penny-a-can potato bugs
from Uncle Emil's field.

Autumn is the refrain of the saw rig,
the aroma of sawdust, wealth of a woodpile.
We buy Red Goose shoes with "room to grow,"
tablets with movie stars on the cover,
and yellow pencils Dad will sharpen
with Mother's well-worn butcher knife.

Winter lingers. In the log barn, gentle Holsteins
long for freedom, anxious captives in their stalls.
The frozen manure pile remains our sledding hill;
snow-soaked mittens dry behind the heater stove.
The earthy scent of potatoes sprouting in the root cellar
in time gives way to that of freshly turned soil,
alive with wriggly earthworms,
in the garden of another spring.

Fiction
Kim-Marie Walker

Pancakes and Waffles

"Hey, Des, this is the first time I've had your pancakes in the bush." Mark belched and patted his stomach. He was stuffed with sourdough cakes, sausage, and two over-easy eggs.

"Un-huh, next you'll say you've never had hand-squeezed orange juice in the bush." Desi smiled. "More coffee?"

"Naw, thanks babe, I'm good to go. What are you gonna do all day?"

Desi rolled her eyes. "What I do every day. Watch our children, make this place a home, have dinner ready when you walk through the door."

"Well, it's a long day for me—jet flights from Anchorage have increased. That means more tourists to haul out to lodges on our smaller aircraft."

"Mommy! Where's Daddy?"

Out the door to another life, she thought, before replying, "He just left to go fly his plane. Good morning, sleepy-head. Want some pancakes?"

"No, Mommy. I want waffles," Danny replied, wiping his eyes.

"Hon, Mommy can't make waffles."

"Why not?"

"We don't have a waffle iron to make waffles."

"Why not?"

"Mommy didn't bring it to this house. It's in the boxes we put at Aunt Trina's."

"Yeah, but I want waffles. You always make me waffles."

"I only have pancakes. You can have cereal and fruit."

"Waffles, Mom. Please, Mom, please?"

"Danny, I'm . . ."

"But, Mom, why is the waffle thing at Aunt Trina's?"

"Honey. It's there because we couldn't bring everything here. We'll have waffles when we go back home to Anchorage."

"But, Mom, why isn't here home? I want waffles!"

"I cut up some bananas, your favorite."

"Mmm, my favorite. Ba-nan-nas 'n' lots of waffles with lots of syrup." Five-year old Danny looked directly into his mother's eyes. Desi laughed.

The salad and mashed potatoes had been prepared hours ago. A foil-covered meatloaf was inside a turned-off oven. A square pan of yellow cake with chocolate frosting had a couple pieces missing. It was 9:30, past supper time, but Alaska's evening sky was still blue with patchy clouds.

"I won't call. If anything's wrong, they'll call me." Desi heard muffled rumbling. She ran to the entry door. Mark was driving up in a company truck. Desi stayed on the rickety top step, blinking back tears.

"Sorry, sweetie. Tried to make a call when I landed about twenty minutes ago, but the lines were all in use. I had to write up the last flight before leaving."

"I didn't know what to think . . . I was just about to call."

Mark wrapped an arm around her. "Hey, babe, I'm sorry. I had to wait for passengers at a remote lodge. From now on I'll have the dispatchers call you when I'm later than scheduled."

Desi stood behind the airport ticket counter. She'd been hired a few weeks before, to deal with the increase of hunters. The fishing season was over, the hunting season was almost over, and September's daylight decreased every day. Desi thought about recent changes. The flight service Mark worked for offered to keep him through the winter, as part of their flights serving nearby bush communities. Trailer lodging and utilities were still free. There was also talk of moving into a two-bedroom apartment.

Shifting her weight to relieve sore feet, she heard Danny's

high pitched voice.

"Mommy! It's time to go!"

"Hi, Danny. Where's Elisa?" Elisa, the babysitter, walked in with year-old Brandon on her hip. Elisa's mom ran a daycare, so Danny played with kids his age and baby Brandon was well cared for during the two and a half days Desi worked. After punching out from her shift, Desi went to baggage claim for three blue, hard plastic shipping containers her sister had shipped. With the help of a co-worker, Desi hauled the containers into the bed of Elisa's truck. Elisa drove them back to the trailer and, together, they lugged each container inside. After Elisa left, Brandon was content with a juice bottle. Danny wouldn't let up about his race cars, packed somewhere inside a container.

"Look Danny, Aunt Trina really taped these up good. See the duct tape?"

"Mommy, there's no ducks. Hurry up, please!" The first container was full of winter clothes and boots. Danny's cars were on top in the second one.

When Mark arrived home, the smoky aroma of bacon met him at the door.

"Hey, Des. Smells good."

"We're having waffles tonight. By popular demand, mind you."

Danny, racing cars on the kitchen's linoleum floor, looked up and said, "Yeah, Aunt Trina sent the waffle thing. Looks like we're finally home."

Poetry
Lina Belar

At the Chamber Music Workshop

Each day the violinists arise, trek up the hillside
to the practice studios overlooking Lake Superior.

Lagging behind them come the cellists,
lugging instruments on their backs like sherpas.

Breakfast is fruit and muffins and hard-boiled eggs
with sandwiches for lunch you build yourself.

Instead of mustard, Bach is slathered on hard rolls,
a pinch of Vivaldi in the salad, modern composers as relishes.

All day long the musicians practice;
the lake hears them all, makes its own composition.

Creative Nonfiction
Virginia Eckert

Prost (the beginning)

Men are shifty, even the good ones, I thought as I sat next to him at the bar and bought him a shot of Jameson.

He said, "What's that German thing they do? We have to look each other in the eye while we drink." So with the glasses in our hands, we looked at each other as we slowly brought the glasses to our lips and drank.

"Prost," we both said, not breaking eye contact.

He talked to me like he didn't have a girlfriend. With long red hair and even longer legs. Like he didn't know that I knew about her. No hints that she even existed. And, if he were a complete stranger, I never would've known.

I never mentioned my husband either. I guess that makes me shifty too. So then we played like children and made every excuse to touch. And for the time being, our lives outside of this bar didn't exist.

And as we walked out and said goodbye, he hugged me tight, pressing his whole body against mine. And I pressed back.

His mouth was near my ear and he said, "It was nice seeing you again." So close I could feel his breath.

And we ended our embrace and walked away. People are shifty. Even the good ones.

Poetry
Adrian S. Potter

Once Someone You Loved
Becomes Someone You Don't

Squander stretches of time considering what could have been,
though often your musings won't progress past the nostalgia
of a kind gesture or the implicit sweetness of a first date smile.
At times, distance will feel insignificant enough to overcome

but comfortable enough to maintain. You'll light everything afire
just to singe idle thoughts. But when the field of a failed marriage
gets slashed and burned, all you can do is survive as the flames
deposit fistfuls of ash at the back of your throat. Stepping back

from the scorched earth, there are no underhanded intentions
or desires to complicate what should remain simple. After all,
to remain where you're no longer wanted is to render the soul
towards emptiness. To embrace separation would be to shorten

what's causing your pain, dissolving what it means to be tender
in a world where emotion is no longer needed. In what you call
memories, you'll no longer find beauty. A future cannot be made
perfect by comparing it to a flawed history of brilliant mistakes.

Poetry
Susan McMillan

Carnival Ride

In the middle of cold night
motion woke me
as your hand reached
over rumpled blankets
to hold mine

you couldn't see
my smile but maybe
sensed movement on the pillow
from muscles in my face
the thought of us two

alone on a mattress
one minuscule point
on the vast surface of this orb
rotating spinning revolving

Ferris wheel ride
while silver peel of moon
slips among stars
bright carnival lights

millions of miles
from immense molten sun
in deep winter
only your warm hand
to hold me on

Poetry
Marlys Guimaraes

what you need to know about eating a lime

it wrinkles your nose   squints your eyes
and like the first taste of beer   you will spew it out
even as pulp clings hidden under your tongue

you must remember not to squeeze
the juice into your sleeping lover's open mouth

instead chop

a scarlet tomato and a potent onion
the kind that stings your eyes
mince garlic cloves   jalapeno peppers

be careful not to rub your tears

cut the lime in half   squeeze
until juice drips from your fingers
into the bowl   add salt   pepper
and mounds of fragrant chopped cilantro

mix and chill

your fingers will smell of onion and hands burn
from the heat of flaming hot peppers

you wait for your man   cool your fingertips
in a frozen margarita   lime with a salted edge

Stan Getz and Joao Gilberto's samba
haunts empty spaces   you fear that next time
limes   tequila   salsa   tortillas and avocados
crushed   will not bring your lover back

Fiction
Neil Millam Frederickson

Fell Darkness

When Toby finally awoke, it wasn't from a sudden noise but from the sudden silence. For two days, he and Tim had lived with the relentless swaying, the constant sound and feel of the train wheels clicking over the rail joints. When those sensations at long last ceased, he jerked awake, heart pounding, his roughened hand already on the warm wood of his M-14 rifle.

Impenetrable darkness, like swimming through ink.

It had already been sunset when he stretched out on the floor of the roofless gondola car, and it was dark still, as though the black and starless sky had fallen to earth and draped over him like a shroud.

He turned his head to listen. The crickets sang at full throat, so the train must have been stopped for a while. Something moved nearby: Tim awake, on the other side of the car.

A moment later: "Toby?"

"I'm awake," he replied. "Why are we stopped?"

Tim moved over to him, carefully, quietly. "I don't know. We went slower and slower, and finally just stopped."

"No alert? No whistle? No flare?" They spoke in whispers.

"Nothing."

"Shit!"

"Shit, indeed."

Toby hesitated. "Are we alone?"

"Aren't we always?"

They listened with straining ears. Their car was near the end of the train, far from the engine. This far toward the back, they couldn't even hear the diesel engine running. Or not running.

"How long have we been stopped?" Toby asked.

"Only a minute. Well, maybe five minutes. No more than ten minutes, for sure. Time gets kind of weird when you're waiting for something to happen."

"I know."

Toby held the rifle against his chest, taking in the smell of grease. The M-14 was clean and oiled. He felt for the safety with a fingertip, clicked it back and forth several times, and left it on safe. *The tool of my trade.* "What can they possibly be doing?" he asked.

"Hard to tell. Maybe it's a switching place. You know, where the tracks divide. Maybe someone has to move the tracks over."

Toby said nothing for a moment. "I don't like sitting still. It feels safer when we're moving."

"That makes no sense. Every mile we go is a mile farther from safety."

"Actually, that had occurred to me," Toby replied drily. "Do you have any idea where we are?"

"Not a clue. We were going east just before dark. I think we turned north later. It felt like it, anyway."

"Damn it all!" Toby swore. "If it weren't overcast, we could see our direction by the stars." He uncoiled his frame and stood, every joint in his seventy-year-old body crackling. He peered over the edge of the car, taking in the creosote smell of the track ties. "I can't even see the ground." He turned toward the front of the train. Was that a red light up ahead? He blinked, and it was gone. Or had never been there. "I might have seen a red light up front. But maybe not."

Tim did not respond.

"What are we doing here with these yahoos? Hell, we're three times their age." Toby slumped back to the floor and laid the rifle across his knees. "I never thought it would end this way, carrying a gun."

"It's not ended," Tim replied. "Take it easy. Anything could happen."

"And that's supposed to *encourage* me?"

"You know what I mean."

"While you're at it, spare me the 'death be not proud' speech. At the moment, death seems pretty damn mighty and dreadful."

"Let's talk resources. We have our rifles, canteens of water and two days' rations."

"And the radio, although if we use it the battery will run down."

"Toby—"

"And I have the binoculars, but in the dark they're about as useful as tits on a boar hog."

"I'm confident the sun will rise tomorrow, if that's what's worrying you."

Toby snorted. "That's not what I'm worried about. My back could spasm on me, or your knee could go out at any minute."

"Let me finish. We have a compass and a flashlight."

"Which we can't use, or the batteries will wear down."

"I'm saying we have the means to survive and maybe even do some damage."

"I don't want to do any damage. I'd rather go home, pay my taxes, and color inside the lines. I want to sleep late and have interesting dreams."

Tim sighed. "Maybe you should remind me: why are you here?"

Fiction
Alberta Tolbert

Father

I conjure you, my father.

Your calloused hand tosses corn to a half-dozen hens. In this soundless world, corn falls silently on dew-drenched grass. Behind you, the once-red barn tilts—weathered and gray—dilapidated in your absence.

I walk to you in slow measured steps. Perhaps this time you will be different. Your cold eyes turn away.

My power to hold you is dissipating. Soon you will disappear into the approaching mist.

It is time.

My voice cracks as if unused in a lifetime. "Did you ever love me?"

"I raised you. Wasn't that enough?"

Fiction
Adrian S. Potter

These Things Happen

It's Christmas time. You and your mother battle through a crowded department store. Unsupervised kids flood the toy section. Some misbehave—yanking action figures out of their packaging, pointing water guns and plastic swords at each other, shrieking and sprinting through aisles as if they were at an indoor playground.

You see a neon mini-basketball. Without thinking you snatch it off the shelf and dribble twice on the linoleum, which registers as a blip on the commotion scale compared to the hubbub of the other children.

Still, Mama scowls and pulls you aside. You hear the subtle venom in her voice as she hisses, "Boy—don't do things that will get you noticed. People are already watching you. You're black."

*

After a meeting, a co-worker laments about his struggles to repair his home computer. Since you're a bit of a tech geek, you kindly offer to stop over after work and help.

To your surprise, you are told that you would not be welcome in his house. He says, as a matter of fact, you would not be welcome in his neighborhood because of the old mindset that exists there.

From then on, you keep your distance in the office. But weeks later you overhear him, again bellyaching about the same computer issue. You laugh to yourself. Old mindsets evidently can't fix modern problems.

*

The media has made it trendy, but "diversity" is slowly becoming a hollow word. A void. People ask you to fill that void. You turn into the void. This is called being accepted. You're supposed to like it. Breathe easy. Exhale.

*

"But some of my best friends are black," he says with a pretentious smirk, as if this unproven statement exonerates him from any damage caused by his reckless remarks. Or as if people who claim to be open-minded maintain an inventory of friendships categorized by race, religious background, sexual preference, etc.

You look at your hands, already squeezed into eager fists, your mind entertaining the dare of punching his face—if only to test his hypothesis, to verify whether any of the buddies who would rescue him from an ass-whipping are indeed black.

The first punch lands squarely on his jaw.

*

A man outside of the parking ramp is asking for handouts.

Normally you're at least good for the loose change in your pocket, but he's wearing a T-shirt embossed with a Confederate flag. Your right hand reflexively probes inside your pocket for coins, but your eyes are continuously drawn towards the symbol of your ancestors' enslavement on his chest. So you walk past, wordlessly.

*

There's one other black guy in your company, Greg, and by chance you start at the firm on the exact same day. Soon you grow tired of correcting people, so sometimes you answer to the wrong name. You get accustomed to saying "no worries" when you're mistaken for another man who you look nothing like. Maybe you even flash a smile, make the older, white managers feel more comfortable about their blunder. "It's no big deal." How could they be expected to see us both as individuals? To see the differences between us, their two quota fillers, the twin tokens, the dual diversity statistics?

You're an optimist and overachiever, so you assume the mistaken identity issue will eventually wane. At some point during your careers, people will figure out who is who. An awesome performance or terrible blunder will distinguish one of you from the other. Time passes and the name mix-ups do still happen, but less frequently.

During an office event, supervisors hand out plaques and accolades to employees who have been working there ten years or more. A decade at a job is a big deal, and you're humbly proud of this achievement. You and several others stand in front of the remaining staff and receive awards and kind applause. You are silently relieved that no one prods you into giving an awkward impromptu speech. Towards the end of the festivities, you look down and realize the name on the plaque you're holding is not yours.

You and Greg swap plaques afterward, away from everyone else. You both laugh it off, but neither of you finds it funny. Greg makes a halfhearted excuse for their mistake and then says flatly, "These things happen."

And yes, it's true, these things do happen. But they really shouldn't.

Poetry
Janice Larson Braun

The Next Morning

You wake up
And discover Sadness,
Small and grey,
Has burrowed its way
Into your heart.
Your eyes burn.

And in that spot
Just above your belly
Where you carry Hope,
There now lies
Coiled
And knotted
Something new and unnamed.

Fiction
Audrey Kletscher Helbling

Grocery Shopping

Belle slipped into the grocery store, head down, focused. She wanted only to secure the items he demanded and some fruit, then leave.

She shoved the cart down the aisle toward the meat counter. "Get a steak, three pounds of hamburger, brats, buns," he ordered. One steak. None for her.

In the produce section she skirted oranges, lobes of grapes and clamshells of blackberries while pushing toward the bananas. Belle dropped a clump into the cart, uncaring. The bananas were already bruised. Nothing mattered anymore.

In the bakery, she scooped a half-dozen bagged hamburger buns from a shelf. "White, not that whole wheat crap," he said.

She passed the floral department where $2 bargain sweetheart roses bunched in buckets. A memory flashed of pink roses and sweet words. "You are so beautiful. Beautiful," he whispered. "You will always be mine. I chose you." She believed him.

But months later his words cut like knife blades. "You're worthless, lazy, ugly," he shouted. She listened, silent and cowering, legs tucked under a fleece throw. Belle blamed herself. He was overworked, tired, stressed. She would try harder.

And so she did whatever he asked of her. Picked up the steak, the ground beef, the brats, the buns. Bypassed the tempting fruit for bruised bananas. She loved him.

Yet, the weight of his anger pressed on Belle as she wheeled up to the check-out counter. "Hi, how are you?" the clerk asked. "Did you find everything you need?"

Belle ignored the greeting, mumbled that she'd forgotten

something. He needed ketchup. She turned and hurried toward aisle three. As she grabbed a ketchup bottle by the neck, Belle felt panic squeeze her airway. She willed herself to breathe, to return to the checkout lane, to parcel out the bills and coins he had tossed at her.

She had everything he wanted. But she knew it wasn't enough, that he would accuse her of spending too much, of buying the wrong cut of steak or the wrong brand of ketchup. Belle would shut down then, pull inside herself and wait for his hand to rise.

Later she would fry his burger just as he liked—rare. Then ketchup, red as blood, would seep through his fingers and pool onto his plate.

Poetry
Louise Bottrell

Jungled

The age-old story of romance

       lost in the feeling
       the feeling lost

Verse follows verse
Page upon page

Whittle it down, I'm told
Remove redundant & repetitious
Words & phrases & stanzas
Erase the inane & the banal, the stale

I labor incessantly
One could say obsessively

finally, I have it

      you   *Tarzan*

      me   *Jane*

Poetry
Peter Stein

Unmoved Mover

I used to think I could push
      back against the earth to alter its orbit

Now I bow as it blows wind
      and wonder what to say

To the wall I built
      that falls to my feet

Do I brace it with my arms
      to be buried by its weight?

No, I stand back, let it
      crash into the unmoved earth

Too crushed to tell it
      I told you so.

Fiction
Charmaine Pappas Donovan

Ring of Fire

The lyrics of Johnny Cash's song playing on the radio drew Jenni's attention to her hand. "Ring of Fire." She'd worn the ring for years. Guilt, its own kind of burn. She snatched a list from the dining room table and drove to the store. Her veins stood out like exposed tree roots. Hadn't she read in *Redbook* that a woman's hands gave away her age?

In her prime she met Greg during a rodeo. He was riding a mustang named Ringo. She watched him win the team roping competition with his brother Earl. Greg was tall and wiry, though graceful and quick, both on and off his feet. He'd lassoed her like a pro.

Within weeks they fell in lust, then married after she found out she was pregnant with Rachel. The thin band on her finger reminded her of the promise she broke. She was as tied up in guilt as that steer Greg roped at the rodeo. Irma, an old woman she'd cared for around that time, became too weak to walk. One day she wiggled the band from her pudgy finger. "See that my granddaughter Claire gets this." Her hand shook as she put the gold band in Jenni's hand. Jenni eloped and moved in with Greg the week Irma died.

Irma's ring went from Jenni's pocket onto her finger. Greg always promised her a real ring, but after he bought cigarettes and whiskey, he barely had enough money to pay bills. If he'd done shift work instead of working on ranches, maybe they would have stayed married. Someone saw his arm around another woman. One weekend when he didn't return to their apartment, Jenni moved back home.

After the breakup, Greg showed up sporadically to see their

daughter. He always wore his cowboy boots, the soles caked with manure. Jenni began to notice the smell of booze on his breath. She shook her head as she said, "No, you can't take Rachel in your car." He frowned. "You visit here." He roared off that day in a cloud of dust, backing his dented Roadrunner down her parents' driveway. A year later Jenni got the call that a hit-and-run driver knocked the boots off Greg as he walked along a rural road where his car ran out of gas.

Raising Rachel and helping her aging parents kept Jenni busy. Thank goodness her folks lived until after Rachel completed college. They drove west in Jenni's SUV to attend the graduation ceremony, celebrating at a local sports bar. Jenni buried her parents within a year of each other. She lived in their rural home until she tired of planting and weeding the perennials, snow-blowing and shoveling. She owned a town home when she learned that Irma's granddaughter lived next door.

Why hadn't she returned that damn ring? When Jenni moved back in with her parents, to the same town where Irma's daughter lived, she thought about going over there. But what would people think? No one would hire her if they knew she was a thief. For years she worked as a bookkeeper at the granary. No, she had to keep sleeping in the bed she made.

Jenni met Irma's granddaughter, Claire, at a picnic when their townhouse association gathered for its semi-annual meeting. Claire invited Jenni to a bible study, an invitation she accepted. Both were widows. When the church planned a tour of Italy, they talked of rooming together.

But not before she told Claire the truth. Jenni placed the ring on the table. Her heart lurched like a tiger ready to leap through a fiery hoop as she punched Claire's number into the phone. As she invited Claire for coffee, Jenni gazed at the plaque Claire had given her: "Lord help me to remember that nothing is going to happen to me today that You and I, together, can't handle."

Scanning Jenni's face as she opened the door, Claire said, "What's wrong?"

Jenni gestured for Claire to sit down, then poured coffee. "Claire, years ago I kept what wasn't mine." Jenni opened her hand. "This ring belongs to you." She explained Irma's dying wish was for Claire to have the ring and how Jenni came to keep it. "I've felt like a criminal ever since."

Silence. Then laughter. "Oh, Jenni, Grandma never liked me. She left me that ring because I was her only granddaughter. You keep it." Claire grasped Jenni's hands. "As a symbol of our forever friendship."

Poetry
Chet Corey

My Summer Find
A cottonwood stump
as flat and round
as a tabletop for two.

0 to be seven again
in love with a
girl who has a tea set!

Poetry
Kate Halverson

Sleeve Pocket

he says only once
in the middle of the night

my wrestling sheets
and layered pillows
awake before light

Tuck your fingers into my sleeve
he prods to settle me down with his
sweet, yet odd suggestion

I blame the full moon before
sleeve pocket does the trick—
a tender cuddle-me moment
midnight fix

Poetry
Dawn Loeffler

Un-whined
You
flip and flop
the most
innocent
sincere
comment
into a moral crisis
a liquid resentment
so distorted
it is unrecognizable

You
bat it around
beating to death
the essence
until it is newly formed
to your jaded influence
finally
spat
upon the page
proof of my defiance

When
in fact
it was quite simply
a parting of ways

Poetry – Honorable Mention
Susan McMillan

Midnight Blue

I'd like to coax
from behind those stars
some of that midnight blue,

spill it in a glass, guzzle it down,
get me a voice
like a nightclub diva—

warm and sad, low and slow,
put on some grooves
sort-of sexy and smooth,

not be so uptight and shy.
Spin me in spangled
stiletto shoes

till I let go,
drift the flow of that dark
cool river of dream

and be a little bit bad.
For one short night, let me be
just a little bit bad.

Fiction – Honorable Mention
Cindy Fox

Mistakes

Our parents never talked about what happens when you leave home.

Fueled for flight, you'll hit the open highway. You'll ignore the double yellow strip on the pavement and pass slow-moving cars with old people who seemingly have no place to go. Recklessly, you'll drive, never looking in the rearview mirror at what you left behind.

Dusty gravel roads behind you, the big city's future will be an open gateway, arms spread wide, beckoning you to drive in. But you'll be ill-prepared, leaving the farm with only forty dollars, which Dad so proudly tucks in your pocket. You'll be grateful your girlfriend's parents let her leave after graduation, unlike you who had to work on the farm until the grain harvest was done. She'll have found a tiny apartment to rent, just enough room for two. Though the windows face the adjacent building's brick wall, you'll both agree privacy from prying eyes is more important than a view of the city's skyline.

No money for the bus, you'll trudge the streets of downtown Minneapolis, applying for secretarial jobs. Your search will end when you enter a bank that will hire you because you'll accept a tad over minimum wage. You'll be scared to death at your second interview with a lady looking down on you, half-glasses perched on the tip of her nose. She'll tell you she's giving you the job because you grew up on a farm and know how to work hard. She'll be taking a chance on you. You better not let her down.

You'll have your own job in the big city. You'll feel like you're on top of the world, ready to experience all the good stuff you missed in your last eighteen years. But the city will be the place where bad stuff happens to naive country girls like you.

You'll flirt with boys at beer parties and, later, run and hide under a car to elude their unwanted intentions. You'll invite new boys to your apartment, trusting everyone like you did back home. After work the next day, you'll open your door and feel like you were socked in the stomach. The new console stereo you'd only had for two months will be gone. The loss of your first major purchase will unnerve you each time you make an installment payment for the empty space against the wall. They will not take your David Banks glamour photograph with your long shiny hair and bare shoulders that now sits on the flattened carpet, slightly angled towards your girlfriend's picture, just like you left them that morning atop the console. They never wanted you; they wanted someone who would play their music.

In that same apartment, a boy will coerce you to sample LSD. Terrified, with no way to stop the psychedelic collisions crashing inside your brain, you'll regret getting on this roller coaster that spins you out of control. White-knuckled, you'll ride it out through the darkness of night. When the morning's light promises a new day, a spark of common sense will tell you to never do this again.

You'll think you learned from your mistakes, but around the corner you'll drive to a fork in the road. No human GPS will tell you which way to go, so sometimes you'll take the wrong turn. But you'll learn and learn. With each mistake, you'll learn.

I don't want to preach, little sister. Maybe the city won't lure you in, but should you decide to go, I hope my mistakes will guide you down a safer path. If you ask for my advice, I will tell you when you drive home for a weekend, don't tell Mom and Dad about the bad stuff. Only the good stuff. If you find yourself stumbling in my footsteps, tell them your spacious apartment with its panoramic view is safe and secure. Make sure you tell them you were hired at the largest bank in Minneapolis because you are a farm kid. The pride shining on their faces will be worth all the innocence you lost in the big city.

Poetry
Cheryl Weibye Wllke

Inside
there's a pink, silk scarf flirting
in Twilight's breeze. Spits
of sweat sizzling between
a skyline's nighttime lights.
An outdoor stage of long-legged players
giddy on booze and blues. Inside
there's a poem waiting
to be written. Waiting to make its way
onto the street: dizzy with perfume
and words that turn
heads and elicit a whistle
or two.

Poetry
Elizabeth Weir

Irony

Pillars soar to the portico,
where blind Justice holds high
her impartial scales. In the set

perfection of the Supreme Court
gardens, a mockingbird
casts his song over

starry dogwoods. White pansies,
brilliant in dulled light, nod
to the pock of constant rain.

Blossom-smothered azaleas
froth around a marble bench,
heavy with a man, huddled

under sodden blankets.

Fiction
Andrew O'Kelley

Dave's Diner

I give the table a swipe and shove a chair in with my hip.
When I get to the pass-through, Lou is wiping his face with a
dirty towel but the breakfast rush is almost over. The flat top
hisses like an old radio.

"Cakes, sausage, eggs over-easy," I tell him. He nods and
bends to the lower fridge. I pour a cup of coffee and add a splash
of cream that sinks into the inky black without a trace. I grab
some napkin-wrapped silver and a saucer and take the coffee to
the booth by the front window. I think about working up a smile
but the guy's got his head inside the paper, so I don't bother.
Instead, I study the logo reversed on the glass of the window. It
seems to read differently every day, like a horoscope. Today, I see
"renteD saveD" which is bullshit. I've been renting my trailer for
three years and haven't saved a dime yet. The man lowers his
paper and nods.

I clear a nearby table and scoop the cash into my apron. I
don't count it, but it looks a bit light on the tip. There's a jar on
my dresser at home showing too much clear glass to get me back
to Michigan. Dave said he couldn't afford a raise and his eyes told
me it was true, even though he turned away quick. He's been good
to me, I guess, but only good and I don't know how to trust a guy
like that.

I ring the cash into the old register and see Lou twist a
burner to a tall blue flame. My knees go spongy, and I look away. I
can still see the big, black shadow burned into the paneling in
Tommy's bedroom, the angry pink welts on his tiny fingers, his
eyes pained with the realization that it wouldn't be the last time
he'd hurt his mother. I feel the void in my gut that our rental

deposit used to fill. My stomach flips and I put a hand on the counter. He'd found the matchbook in a kitchen drawer. Maurice's —Florida's Finest Girls it said on the cover. I can see the neon from inside the smoky red club, "see duN eviL" it always scolded. It's ten miles east, down the highway, but Tommy's entire lifetime is behind me now.

Lou sets a plate in the pass-through, his eyes sweeping my face then down to my dirty apron that didn't get washed last night 'cause I fell asleep on the couch, my spare stuffed into the open drain pipe left behind by an unreliable plumber. "Sewer gas," warned a neighbor though it smelled no worse than the diner.

"You okay?" asks Lou, and leans his sweaty face into the rectangular opening, his plump fingers gripping the edge. I glance over and lose hope in his hopeful expression.

"Yeah, I just—I'm fine." I grab a bus pan and clear a few vacated tables. A pair of older women shuffles out the door, hard shoes scraping the worn linoleum. Their tip is all change, counted exactly to ten percent. If the menu and decor haven't changed in their lifetime, why would their tip? The front window says, "run ID's evaDe."

"Jesus," I think. "I'm not exactly on the lam." But I'd hold up a liquor store if I thought the old Valiant could make it all the way to Momma's hospice in Dearborn.

I reach the booth by the window. I hadn't seen the guy leave but his plate is empty. The newspaper lies folded beside it and tucked beneath is a hundred dollar bill. I slide the dishes into my bus pan, put the bill in an empty pocket of my apron and look out the front window. No one on the sidewalk outside. The diner is empty. I head for the kitchen and then turn back to the window again. "Dave's Diner" is all it seems to say.

Fiction
Kevin Zepper

Empress

The tattooist inked in the final few brush strokes in the raised black border of the tiny heart. The red ink and droplets of blood were indistinguishable from one another.

It was an innocent design, usually found on an ankle or inside thigh of an older sister or a mother, as a remembrance or dare. Modesta giggled quietly; this was the last one. She misjudged the amount of skin space she had, but it's not easy measuring with a mirror and a tailor's tape. Her tiny laugh was also an acknowledgment of a new freedom: one she had held her breath for her whole life.

Modesta rarely looked in the mirror at herself and was horrified of showing the least bit of her skin. She was a remarkable flower, but kept herself under clothing, her hands gloved, face covered when she went out. Her childhood physicians said she had no skin disorder—perfectly healthy skin. Her fear of seeing her flesh frightened her; the thought of anyone seeing her nude was as horrifying to her as breaking a sacrament.

In the months prior to the heart tattoo, she grew more comfortable with this new skin of choice. No longer pale and pink, it was a narrative tapestry of every image she took delight in: a turquoise waterfall, a Morgan Horse, a church belfry, a patch, a piece of illuminated scripture. It was all there and more.

When the tattooist finished, he wiped off the needle and wept. Modesta removed her drop cloth from her lap. With her remaining bare skin covered in color, she exited the shop, exhaling relief deeply from her lungs, walking straight and tall, her new colors covering every naked space of her former blank canvas, until she disappeared into the scenery of the street.

Poetry
Meridel Kahl

Beatles 1965-66

I went to a school founded
by Norwegian Lutheran immigrants

at the top of a wind-swept
Minnesota hill

where autumn sunsets
bled fuchsia, gold, dark-velvet purple

and my heart ached
with something I couldn't name.

That spring I moved on
in search of new rhythms

like sweet-energy
Liverpool music,

full of key changes
edgy with surprise.

Fiction
Jennifer Hernandez

Fungible

"We want our teachers to be fungible."

The principal strutted across the front of the cafeteria, his staff seated uncomfortably at lunch tables spread in rows before him. *Like cartons of eggs,* he thought.

"This new curriculum tells you exactly what to say, exactly what to do at each step of the lesson. No guesswork involved. It won't matter if a student is in Ms. Johnson's class or Mr. Castillo's. They'll be learning the exact same material in the exact same way. Fidelity is the key. Our test scores will catapult into *meets and exceeds* territory."

He beamed out at the assemblage of teachers before him. He'd been told that the previous principal lacked vision, lacked the fortitude to make the changes that needed to be made. There was even talk that the teachers had been on the verge of a strike. He was here to put things right. Looking out at the motley group, many slouching over their coffees, whispering to their neighbors, doing paperwork, on their phones, he shook his head inwardly. He had his work cut out for him. That much was clear.

"I googled it," said one teacher near the back, rising from her seat. "Fungible. It means interchangeable. He wants us to be cogs in the machine."

"Exactly!" He grinned. "You've got it!"

"Well then, consider me the wrench."

Poetry
Dianne M. DelGiorno

College Teaching 101

So much depends upon
    what you do
        and undo
what you say
    and what
        your body
      language leaves
        unsaid
      to the constellation
        of students
you pass through
    before you put
        your key
    in their
        classroom door.

Fiction
Kathryn Knudson

At the Edge of the Junkyard

"You're sure they can't hear us?" I whispered, swatting another mosquito. Apparently new perm smell wasn't much of a deterrent.

Dean replied casually, as if we weren't crouched behind a junked car spying on a field party. "Nah. We're, like, half a mile away."

I raised an eyebrow he couldn't see in the dark. The football players from our rival town were closer to a hundred yards from the junker.

Beside me Kimberly sighed. "I'm so bored."

Someone's boombox played "St. Elmo's Fire."

For about the twelfth time I wondered why I'd agreed to join her new boyfriend, Craig, and his best friend, my cousin Dean, instead of watching *The NeverEnding Story* on her brand new VCR. But Craig was a sophomore, and Kimberly, cutest girl in our class, was the only eighth grader dating one, so here we were.

Dean waved around binoculars he'd swiped, probably from my parents' store.

"Just wait; it'll get more interesting. "

That didn't sound good. He'd told us "the penny ante bullshit" between the towns ended tonight. If my parents found out we were with Dean instead of sleeping over at Kimberly's, my life would be ending tonight.

"Why?" Kimberly now sounded more worried than bored. "What'll they be doing?"

Craig piped up. "They'll be being sorry. That's what they will be doing."

Good grief. My eyes rolled.

"Vodka, baby?" Craig offered.

My eyes rolled again.

I felt Kimberly reach for the bottle.

"Are you crazy?" I grabbed her wrist, column of jelly bracelets shifting beneath my hand.

Kimberly shoved the bottle back. I had a feeling she was a lot pissed and a little relieved but, before she could say anything, Dean shifted.

"Holy shit, hear that?" He practically cackled.

We listened. Now it was "We Built This City" but that wasn't what he meant. Between us and the party, we heard quietly shutting car doors. Lots of them. Then, slowly, swishing grasses in the ditch. Suddenly the horizon lit up with careening flashlight beams, even a floodlight. Men started shouting commands. Deputies.

Our heads popped up.

Shit, even deputies from the next county. Kids scrambled. Shrieked. Doors slammed. A truck tried to turn over.

Dean's face was glued to the binoculars. "Look at 'em run. Scared little pussies."

Whoa. No wonder my parents thought he was Bad Influence.

"I can't get a good look at their faces," he muttered. "It's still so goddamned dark."

"That's what happens at night," Craig cracked.

Kimberly giggled.

Yeesh.

Dean lowered the binoculars.

Craig slouched. "Sorry, man."

I practically felt Kimberly's interest drop.

More yelling. Thrashing through the cornfields. Swearing. Crying. Lots of crying. It felt terrifying and kind of sad. I touched Kimberly's arm; we slid down onto the dirt. I just wanted it to be over.

"What'd you do, Dean?" I asked quietly.

He laughed, mean and hard.

"Someone might've heard Stephanie Hendrickson yapping at the gas station. And might've called the sheriff, telling him this little party would have more than just beer. Watch them try to get us back from jail. Dicks."

I looked over to his silhouette. He was really, really enjoying this.

"They have pot here?" Craig sounded astonished.

"No, numbnuts. But the sheriff doesn't know." That mean laugh again.

How could I be related to such a jerk?

"Are you an idiot?" I blurted. "This isn't going to end anything. They'll be back home in a few hours. And want revenge. On our town. You didn't *end* anything. You took this stupid feud and turned it into a war."

Dean turned slowly to me. When he spoke, his voice was very low. "Maybe. Maybe not. What do you know, Jojo?"

I should have been scared but instead I felt anger. "I know someone's going to have to deal with what happens, and I bet it won't be you."

"Who will it be?" He snorted. "You?"

"Yeah, maybe it will." My mouth seemed to have a life of its own. "And then won't your pansy ass be surprised that a fourteen-year-old girl did what you couldn't."

This time he barked out a long laugh, deputies and chaos forgotten. "I'll believe it when I see it."

And he did.

But that would be months down the road. After they retaliated. After things got worse. After Kimberly was gone.

Tonight he just clutched those binoculars until the last truck was towed away, and we were left back in the dark with the mosquitoes.

Poetry
Jennifer Hernandez

The River
that ran behind our house
was forbidden. It swallowed children
we learned that November,
as we watched out the back window
while divers searched for the body
of the neighbor boy who sledded
down the hill onto not-thick-enough
ice and drowned. Delicate, crackling skin
gave way. River opened his mouth
to accept the offering.

We kept our distance from the River.
Threw rocks in and sticks
that floated away with the current.
Calm on the surface, but
parents warned of stronger swirls,
eddies that lurked
waiting to grab ankles, pull us below,
toss and turn, never let go. Until
we, too, were cradled deep in the mud
of the riverbed, food for bottom feeders
with whiskered puckering mouths.

Fiction
Deb Schlueter

Sculptures

The rolling suitcase bounced as the woman dragged it up the dirt road, her crimson jacket bright against a blue sky and pine trees. She looked like someone that should be parading through a fancy airport—not walking down a forest road. The school bus passed her, kicking up a cloud of dust.

"Who's that?" asked a boy on the bus, craning his head around to see her.

"She moved into the old house on the hill a few weeks ago," another kid said. "Dad said to ignore her; she's just a crazy city person."

A few minutes later, the boy got off the bus and lingered outside, away from the looming trees that cast dark shadows on his house. She came into view again, walking like a model on a runway, her black hair in a braid threaded with silver, a yellow wildflower tucked into a buttonhole of her jacket, her shoes coated in dust. She didn't seem to notice him as she passed by.

Just beyond his driveway she paused, gazing into the ditch. Leaving the road, she stepped through the weeds to pick something up. Back at the road, she unzipped her suitcase, set the object inside, zipped her bag back up, and continued on her way.

His forehead wrinkled. Leaving his backpack at the mailbox, the boy followed her, peering into the weeds: scattered feathers from a long-dead bird. He glanced back toward his house, then picked up his pace until he was walking next to the old woman.

"What'cha doing?" he asked.

She didn't answer. He trailed next to her, studying the wrinkles on her hands and the lines on her face. Alter a few ignored questions, he slowed down and followed in her footsteps, watching curiously as she picked up more things to put in her suitcase. Rocks. Sticks. An old can. Leaves. Flowers. A piece of half-rotted paper.

When they reached the old house on the hill, the lady turned up the driveway. He hovered at the edge of the road before chasing after her. "Hey, Lady," he said as they walked towards a small house lost in the grasp of ancient pine trees.

Instead of answering or heading inside, she turned on a small path around the edge of the house. Squirrels chattered and raced around in the trees as the boy followed and found himself stopped by a fence. The gate clanged shut behind her. He leaned against the wood, stretching to see over.

Metal sculptures danced in the breeze in her small backyard. Sunlight glinted off silver and steel and bits of colored glass. "Wow," he whispered.

"You've come this far, might as well come in," the lady said, a slight southern lilt to her gruff voice.

The boy pushed through the gate, studying the sculptures. They were intricate wind catchers, covered in metallic leaves, flowers, and feathers. Stuff that was supposed to be junk. "What are you doing?" he asked again.

Taking things out of her suitcase, she arranged them on a table in the center of her garden. "Art." She picked up a feather in her long fingers, turning it this way and that in the sunshine.

Fingers laced behind his back, he watched as she pressed the feather into a block of clay, leaving an impression behind. "My friend's dad thinks you're crazy."

Her fingers paused.

"But these are too pretty to be made by a crazy person."

A morose smile drifted onto her face as she looked around her yard. "Maybe your friend's dad is right. Me trying to fill a hole with sculptures."

"Huh?" He crept just a bit closer, daring to pick up a leaf.

"I lost someone up here; I'm trying to find him." Plucking the leaf from his fingers, she said, "You should run along home before you get lost, too."

"I'm not going to get lost." He laughed. She glanced at him, but didn't respond. He hung around for nearly an hour, watching, unable to get her to say another word. "I'm gonna come back this weekend," he said before heading out the gate.

The shadows over his house stretched darker and longer than earlier. Snagging his backpack, he slowly walked up the steps and vanished inside.

Poetry
Steven R. Vogel

Dewberry

There is so little time. The dewberry has fallen,
the peach blossom moth is stark on her red leaves.
The mists have gotten up from the ground
and placed themselves in heaven. Nothing will remember
you whispering after lost children, their toys in a cupboard,
its pine quiet as the day it was planked.
The little trails in the old grass will overwinter,
and perishable legs will renew them many times
before I tire of your pacing the garden lanes,
the hostas lapping at the lace of your anklets,
at the tiny violets stitched into them by hands translated
long ago. But come indoors. Put your slippers aside,
let the dust chase itself, and let the time be now.

Poetry
Sharon Harris

Touch
out in public
lots of people moving

I see you
you see me
as you approach

we can't stop
we don't speak

our eyes don't dare
to meet

but you touch me
as you pass

one knowing finger
runs down my forearm

just lightly brushing
along my skin

your finger moves
with no haste

sliding a white hot path
that I feel everywhere

Creative Nonfiction
Annamae Gunsolus-Holzworth

Four Bells

Without fail, Mae struggled with jet lag when traveling outside of the Central Time Zone. In bed just before midnight on her first night in Lucerne, Switzerland, she awoke at 3:52 a.m., thinking it was time to get up. Relieved that she had more time to sleep, she sank back into the warm feather bedding.

Street light glow illuminated silhouettes of Swiss cows and goats painted on the wall. Her window open, she could hear an occasional car drive by, splashing standing water. The bell of a nearby church tolled four times. A bell in the distance echoed faintly. Midway, a third bell pealed. Mae smiled when her Timex digital watch chirped once. She hoped to sleep until the seven o'clock performance.

Poetry
Georgia A. Greeley

Friends

His given name
wasn't Hummingbird.
He chose it.
You could say
we met on a massage table,
or several massage tables—
which quickly moved us past naked,
past body image,
into a touching space,
which accepts warts and bumps
and hairy legs.
I didn't care he was gay
and he didn't care
I wasn't, as we both learned
how to knead and stretch and ease
our own and others' aching flesh,
connecting underneath
the sheets and towels,
which absorbed the slippery oils
and unnecessary words.

Fiction
Lisa M. Bolt Simons

Pieces

The black and white photograph, the size of a poster, sits dusty and old in one of the FREE! bins at a garage sale this past summer. The woman sitting behind the table says, "I'm not sure who they are, but they look like they're having fun. Probably Leroy's cousins or somethin'."

Leroy?

Then she tells me about her back problem, that she can't dance like *that* anymore, then about her daughter who won local dance contests since the age of five, then about her daughter's daughter who still can't walk at nineteen months and how they were doing tests to figure out why. I politely excuse myself, lying that my black Lab is stuck inside my hot car.

It's his first dance. He just turned sixteen and has not yet dated. His dark hair and eyes overshadow his rather large nose, his almost smile lighting his round face. He's wearing a carbon-colored suit and tie and crisp white shirt. Barely sticking out of his pocket is a handkerchief with monogrammed but unreadable initials. Embarrassed, he's showing his camera-happy mother how he can dance with a woman. It's the Jitterbug—the pace makes her fall back. Her right leg comes up slightly, almost kicking. His slightly cupped left hand barely touches her abdomen, his ignored silver watch not catching delicate skin. His right arm is behind her, stopping the fall.

She is older, a family friend visiting from college. She holds onto him with much more comfort and experience. Her long, fair hair is tied at her neck, bangs reaching past her slightly plucked eyebrows. She looks down for a moment, and the camera catches her when she blinks. She's laughing. Fingernails are short and a deep color. Lipstick and eyeliner enhance her face. A clump of what looks like gold pieces covers her ear. Her dress looks gray, a linen fabric, boat neck, short sleeves, size ten. The fast dancing has made the knee-length dress creep up into several folds, garter belt just showing. Her left bicep rests on his higher shoulder—the bracelets sliding down to rest by his cheek—and her unseen hand grasps his jacket, pulling him close as she loses her balance. The blurry right hand has an oblong, ebony jeweled ring that covers the bottom half of her ring finger, a gift from a former boyfriend.

They are dancing in his home, the Christmas tree behind them almost hidden in shadow, but a metallic ball glimmers from the bottom bough, the air thick with its smell. It's about 7 p.m.

They enjoy the evening. He and his parents accompany her and her parents to the door. The parents decide the couple should get together for New Year's, and she says, "I'll call you." Years later, when he phones his mom from some college close to home, he finds out she's getting married to a bank vice president.

Or maybe the couple gets together after all.

I wonder if she ever got pedicures, let her granddaughter wear the gray dress for Halloween. I wonder if he ever felt comfortable holding his wife's hand in public, whose father he became, if he made enough money for retirement. I wonder if they lived happily ever after.

I put the photograph back behind my computer, her laughing face and his boyish grin just above the screen as I focus on my next story, avoiding the *Romeo and Juliet* essays I promised I'd grade by Tuesday. My fingers rest on the computer keys as I try and force myself to forget that they could be my parents. I was told my mother had blond hair, lighter than mine, whose one blue eye and one green eye caused people to stare. My father wore half a suit once, matching his dark hair, his body framed by his black casket; since the top half of him was the only part visible, his mom didn't buy the matching pants. Can't I imagine the young man in the photograph with his chivalry and pocket handkerchief made a life for himself, selling insurance or becoming a pediatrician, wearing full suits to conferences and lectures and award banquets?

After my parents' deaths and I moved in with my aunt, she tried to tell me bedtime stories not of a teacher or administrative assistant, not of an accountant or business owner but of a prince and princess, riding off into the sunset, living happily ever after.

Poetry
Norita Dittberner-Jax

Reverie

A long spring, a slow
unfolding of leaves small as raindrops,
a night tender with sparrows.

In the back of your closet
are letters that hint at such nights,
letters you hide from the children
knowing they will find them.

Poetry
Cindy Fox

Sunday Mourning

On that Sunday morning in October
I answered the phone, tucked the
message close to my heart, and
returned the phone to its cradle.

I stumbled down the basement stairs,
filled the washing machine with dark clothes,
crawled up the steps on all fours and
pulled four suitcases from the closet.

Opened them slack-jawed on the bed,
packed dress shirts, underwear, socks,
toothbrushes, and a dress for me.
I polished my children's dress shoes.

Laid out my husband's suit and
slipped a handkerchief in a side pocket.
Wiped off spots from his best tie and
set out his toiletry case.

No thoughts, no memories, no emotions
slowed down my mission until I heard
someone at the door, so sure my husband
and children were home from the park.

Ready to share the news locked inside me,
I swung open the door, leaned against it for support.
My neighbor's smile vanished as my face crumpled.
What's wrong?

My mother died this morning.
We clung to each other, tears flowing,
dark mourning clothes going through
the spin cycle.

Creative Nonfiction
Mike Lein

Strange Barn Fellows

One morning, decades ago, I walked across the crunchy gravel yard to the old barn. Birds were singing in the grove, ducks were quacking in the pasture pond, the sun doing its best to convince us it was spring. I swung open the barn door and stood back, releasing the barn's two occupants after a long winter's confinement. The chicken emerged first. Next came the cat, a small male gray tabby. They sauntered around the farmyard together, the chicken pecking and scratching in the gravel, the cat sliding around the chicken, rubbing against yellow legs and white feathers.

We had moved to the country the summer before, seeking solitude and escape from the rundown rental house in town. We found both in an isolated 1930s farmhouse on a gravel road. A few calves in the barn and a chicken coop full of laying hens were our only neighbors. Late that fall the farmer emptied the cattle from the barn and the hens from the chicken coop. A few days later, a scraggly lone hen appeared, scratching in the dirt around the chicken coop. The dog and I captured her after a chase around the yard and moved her to the barn under squawking protest. There she could fend for herself in the leftover hay until the farmer found time to deal with an escapee. Soon thereafter, a young gray tabby cat appeared on the door step, looking for handouts and friends. I moved him into the barn too, figuring the old structure would provide shelter, warmth and perhaps some mice to supplement kitchen leftovers.

One daylight trip to the barn to deliver scraps held a surprise. I opened the door and found the chicken and the cat snuggling together, burrowed into a nest of loose hay. They quickly separated, like a teenage couple caught making out by snooping parents. As the winter progressed, they became more accustomed to my visits and didn't hide the fact that they had some sort of relationship. Then came the spring visit and the coming out scene.

There's a lesson or two here for people who like deep thoughts. The cat could have ambushed the chicken in the dark of long winter night and dined on fresh meat. Or stayed on one end of the spacious barn. Likewise the chicken could have harassed the cat during the day and found elsewhere to roost at night. They chose to hang together, choosing warmth and companionship over combat and loneliness.

I don't remember what happened to these unlikely companions, brought together through circumstances out of their control. But wherever they disappeared to, they left behind a memory from that morning, a mental picture I haven't lost despite the decades that have passed. On a weathered wood fence rail sits a gray tabby cat and a white hen, fur touching feather, basking in the spring sun together.

Creative Nonfiction
Sharon Harris

The Old Homestead

I have gone back to see the old home place. The farm house has paint peeling on all the outside walls; the screen door is ajar. There is an attached woodshed, still full of firewood. A leaning garage stands nearby and the big barn still touches the sky, now with broken windows gaping.

Inside the house, the old linoleum is torn. The ceiling paint is cracked and puckered from leaks. There is a depressed mustiness in the air.

I walk through the rooms, happy to review old memories but sad to see the changes. I step out onto the screened-in porch. Here the dust from the dirt road coats every single thing. This porch used to reach around two sides of the house—now only a small portion of it remains. The rest of the porch was enclosed when another bedroom was needed as well as a laundry room and a new stairway to the basement.

My steps take me back through the house now, looking at the shapes of the rooms, recalling the way it must have looked. The current kitchen began life much smaller. There was once a different bedroom that had been removed to make the kitchen larger; a bathroom had also been carved out of that space.

If I look closely, I can see all the edges of the old house, the shapes of the original rooms, the remains of the old original homestead, the hopes and dreams of the first builders as they started a life here on the prairie.

Poetry
Georgia A. Greeley

Grandma's Cabin Cellar

It wasn't meant for people,
or tornados, it was meant for food.
Tall trees bending over into "U" shapes,
and branches tickling the ground
sent us there.
Wiping cobwebs off our faces,
we crept slowly down the earthen steps,
one after the other.
We could hear the roar outside, but muffled.
It was as if we were wearing three woolen hats
pulled down over our ears,
instead of T-shirts and shorts, and flimsy house dresses.
The kerosene lantern glinted on the rows of peaches,
beets and plums. I started counting jars
as I held my little brothers close.
Breathing the dusty air, sitting on the dirt floor,
the dark shadows and flickering light, didn't bother them;
they wanted to play.
Roy crawled from lap to lap, oblivious.
Mom fidgeted, worry lines across her forehead,
but she didn't say a word.
Grandma glared at the latch on the doors overhead,
made us move farther into the damp darkness and earthy smells.
I watched a huge spider climb a silken thread
and disappear, listened to my family breathe
in different rhythms, curled my back into the wall,
and prayed. Sand drifted into our hair.
The one set of cellar doors snapped open and shut.
Our lantern blew out.
The earth cradled us in darkness
just long enough.

Creative Nonfiction
Linda Maki

Pig's Head

On Christmas day, Auntie served up an authentic Scandinavian buffet at her annual holiday potluck party. Her front door opened and closed all day as relatives were welcomed, but only between the hours of 1-4 p.m.

The older aunts and uncles held court while sitting in the large wooden breakfast nook or on the worn beige couch and chairs in Auntie's spotless living room. They told us stories of the olden days when "Great Grandma and Grandpa walked fifteen miles to Big Lake every spring carrying Little Johnny on their backs, to get flour and sugar," or "Great Grandpa hooked up the horses to the sleigh on Christmas Eve and rode us all over the fields while we sang Christmas carols." We hung on every word asking, "All you got for Christmas was an orange, one orange?" or "No heat in the upstairs bedrooms? You've got to be kidding!"

"Lunch is ready," Auntie would announce from the kitchen and we all bustled to the dining room where a feast of homemade breads, pickles, potato salad, buttered lefse, Aunt Alice's sugar-sprinkled doughnuts and my grandma's fudge-frosted brownies waited. My same-age cousin Pat and I would rush to get two of Auntie's sandwiches piled high with her special lunchmeat. We would take them to the corner of the breakfast nook and gobble them down.

Year after year the party carried on—the "Tradition" sung about in *Fiddler on the Roof.* One year Pat asked Auntie how she made that delicious lunchmeat. "Oh, it's head cheese," Auntie said. "I buy a pig's head at Ingrebretson's down on Lake Street, they have the best ones, boil it all day, put it through the meat grinder and make it into loaves that I slice up. I know you girls just love it."

"Oh, my god!" we whispered to each other, slinking away and spitting out what we had in our mouths. We discreetly dropped the rest into the garbage pail. For us, it was cheese sandwiches from that day until the last open house Auntie had three years before she passed away.

Poetry
Susan Perala-Dewey

Milkweed
faces autumn in full bloom
November sun frames a
freefall of her last seeds

cupped in winter sunlight
her final paratroopers release
floating skyward

elegant against a graying sky
she stands barren once again
open to Earth's unfolding.

Poetry
Judy Budreau

Eating Chocolate with My Mother

My mother stops me
at the door—
You must take more chocolate
for the road.
In the back of my car
my grandmother's rocking chair
where my mother nursed me as a newborn.
A box of ironed linens, some photographs, a breadboard.
Today I learned these stories, and a few more
she had the energy to tell. She wants me to know,
wants me to remember.
I know this: she is disappearing before my eyes, has
little energy, no appetite.
Returning with the chocolate, she tells me
I can make one last half an hour. When it's almost gone,
oh—the final burst of flavor on my tongue! Her smile is wide
when she drops the gold foil into my palm.

This is what I will remember.

Poetry
Tim J. Brennan

Homebound Communion

My wife volunteers every first Sunday.
I accompany today, stand by the door,
aloof, like a resident, and watch her move
to the elderly, offering Christ to those
unable to approach on their own.

There is a woman sitting by herself
on the front porch, ghosts of leaves
at her feet. I see her through the window.
She doesn't appear to notice anything,
not even the glass-like pine needles wefted
behind the screen from winter's weave.
She looks like she may be buried one day
with rosary beads, maybe a battered teddy bear.

Like she may have been crying recently.
Like the rest of her days are falling down.

Fiction
Chet Corey

Teeth

His grandparents slept in the bedroom his grandpa had been born in, but in separate beds, a worn rug between, the floorboards rutted with dust. They'd known love, but he'd only come to think of that after both had died and he'd inherited the farmhouse and outbuildings, the land sold off years earlier.

Most mornings, as a child of four or five, when he'd stay overnight, he'd crawl into his grandpa's bed. His grandmother would call across the room, "Get up and put the kettle on." And his grandpa would squeeze his upper arm, where he'd said hard work would make a muscle, and call back, "Shut up, you old wind bag." Then he'd wink. It was his grandpa's signal she'd never heard one unblessed word and for him to snuggle beneath the feather tick, warm with the old man's farts and flannel pajamas, astringent with liniment from his arthritic wrists, until she'd call across again. And they'd both roll out—first him, then his grandpa, who would sit on the mattress edge and close his eyes a moment in prayer before standing. What words his grandpa said, he never came to know.

She'd worn a hairnet nightly over aluminum-like curlers, kept her dentures in a water glass—hearing aids laid right ear and left to either side—a Kleenex beneath it all on the bureau, its mirror angled downward, reflecting their three faces back.

His grandfather no longer worked the land. He'd rented out the fields to neighbors across the road a half-mile down. But he kept up the small garden on the sunny side of the farmhouse, the garden she'd kept—better than he'd farmed, she'd said—before glaucoma made planting and weeding unmanageable. But she could pick and gather. Pumpkin, squash, pole beans, tomatoes, carrots, four rows of corn—their harvest.

On the east side by the grove was the family plot where the great-grandparents and great-aunt, who had died at birth, lay buried before laws ruled home burial out. After the funeral director closed the lid on his grandmother's casket and the family stepped back, he remembered, as a boy of twelve or so, seeing the man hand his grandpa a small box. When they'd returned from the graveyard outside of town and everyone had gathered in the kitchen or front room, he'd gone upstairs to see where his grandpa was and caught him sitting on the edge of her bed, her upper dentures in one hand, her lower in his other, the cardboard box on the floor. He looked up and winked. "She won't be biting our heads off without these choppers," he said. But he'd seen a glistening well up in his grandpa's eyes and remembered him running the back of his liver-spotted hand roughly across his cheekbone.

So he knew where to find them—her "choppers"—in the hiding place for valuables beneath a cutout of floorboard at the head of her bed. He told his bride-to-be, who waited out front in the yard, he'd go up for one more look out their bedroom window across the stretch of fields. But his grandma's dentures were what he really wanted—all he wanted out of whatever was left in the old place. He'd no need for twin beds, stripped of their mattresses, revealing their coiled metal springs. He went to the narrow window for one long look.

With her "teeth," as she'd called them, in his pocket, to set beside his grandpa's "choppers," which a much younger funeral director had given him before closing the old man's casket, he started down the stairway, and then out the front door, which they'd seldom used, coming in through the mud room door leading down to the cellar. He stood for a few moments on the front stoop, then headed quickly toward his bride-to-be. She took his arm and they walked toward the car, the bulldozer shuddering mechanically toward the farmhouse.

What he'd do with the both of them—their dentures—he'd no idea. But he knew they should be together. He'd tossed her hearing aids years before. The old man could keep calling back at his old love, graveside to graveside, whenever he wanted. Their separate plots, after all, were like twin beds. And, if in the first light of some morning, his grandpa wanted to give his upper arm a squeeze, that would be okay, too. He'd say the boy had learned to make a muscle.

Poetry
Alan Perry

Leaving

They all left about
the same time
for a final trip together.

Ethel couldn't see unless she
turned her head sideways,
which is how we found her asleep.

Donna inhaled her smoke so
deeply that it pushed
the cancer just behind her nose.

Bob began writing down
every bone he broke, until
pneumonia crept in between the lines.

Bud's heart had miles
of extra plumbing attached,
before it stopped to take a rest.

They likely rode out on a train
in their finest clothes
having a highball in the club car,
smiling at the Western sun.

Poetry
Sarah Cox

Requiem
(David, 1963-2016)

We will plant a tree, at the lake, by the water
　　　He always talked about the trees he planted
　　　In the yard behind his house
　　　(Those interminable phone calls, packed with silence)
　　　We saw the trees
　　　Aspens he brought down from the mountains
　　　Planted along his back fence
　　　Seedlings he nurtured in a raised bed
　　　A single tiny blue spruce, perfect pyramid
　　　Rising from a sea of dead grass
At the lake, by the water, we will plant a tree

We will plant a tree, at the lake, by the water
When the family gathers
　　　Brothers and cousins, nieces and nephews
　　　Those he loved, who loved him
　　　He always brought them gifts
　　　Taught them silly games, splashing in the water
　　　Competing fiercely at tennis, water-skiing
When the family gathers
At the lake, by the water, we will plant a tree

We will plant a tree, at the lake, by the water
When the family gathers, when the summer comes
　　　He always came to us in summer
　　　When the family gathered, at the lake, in the summer
　　　Last year, when he went home, he pushed away his friends
　　　Locked his doors, drank himself to death
　　　It took six weeks
When the summer comes, when the family gathers
At the lake, by the water, we will plant a tree.

Poetry
Marlene Mattila Stoehr

Spurned Heirloom

Among cast-off items donated to
the Second Chance Thrift Shop,
I spied a shallow crystal dish
with a wrinkled note taped inside:
"Your great-grandma Bertha
brought this when she came over
from Germany in 1853."

I grieved for this woman, Bertha,
and for her unnamed descendant
who no longer cared.
What heart can be so small, I agonized,
that it cannot house this object, so valued
more than a century and a half ago?

Then I recalled the words of the poet
who wrote that you shall continue to live
so long as your stories continue to be told.
So I tell you of an ink-stained note,
taped to a crystal dish treasured long ago
by a woman named Bertha.

Poetry – Honorable Mention
Doris Stengel

The Hovering Years

My husband is eighty,
I a couple ticks younger.
We are at that age
where our grown children
have started to hover,
not like vultures,
more like mama birds
protecting their nest.
The house we have lived in
for fifty years is comfortable,
we have come to an understanding.
The children keep bringing up
the lovely "Senior Housing"
available in our town.
We don't want to go there.
The raspberry patch in our backyard
entertains my farm boy husband
for several months each year.
Our dog, probably not allowed
in "housing," takes us for a walk each day.
Our children have begun to hover.
They *are* helpful. They come
to paint, repair, spruce up the house.
I suspect it will sell for a better price.
We truly do appreciate their hovering;
we are just not ready for them to land yet,
because the dust that's accumulating
inside this house, is not yet *us*.

Creative Nonfiction
Kim A. Larson

Change, Anyone?

The only change I like is the kind found at the bottom of a washing machine. I've slept under the same blanket for forty years and in a T-shirt that's only slightly newer. It once displayed my high school's mascot on the front, an Indian, but it's worn so thin it's no longer distinguishable. Which is probably for the best since it's been changed—the mascot, to be politically correct—not my T-shirt. Now we're the Huskies. Even if I did like change, I'd never like being called husky.

Which leads me to my biggest gripe—aging.

Why do bodies have to change? My belly is bigger, my feet flatter. My hair is turning gray, those not falling out. Worse yet, my hairdresser retired. Talk about traumatic! I'm still seeing a therapist.

Once I thought I'd like change if it was *my* idea, so I brought in a picture of Carrie Underwood to have my hair cut like hers. Afterwards, I realized it was her *face* I really wanted and went back to my same old style.

I'm not complaining; it was my choice. However, life's changes aren't always by choice. Yet there's one choice we're always given: how we react to change.

So, I've decided to change—by looking for the positives in change. The most difficult change I've ever gone through is the change of life. The first year of hot flashes made me think the alternative to growing older would be better as I was already being burned at the stake.

With some hard searching, I've even found a redeeming quality in hot flashes. I've never liked getting out of bed in the morning when it's cold. Or hopping into a shower or changing my clothes when it's cold—and it's cold nine months out of the year in northern Minnesota. Now, I just wait for a hot flash before doing those things.

Though perspiring like a sprinkler throughout the day, it's impractical to change soggy clothes that often. My solution was I bought a whole new wardrobe! I needed clothes that could be layered—and rapidly removed. Not all of them, of course, or I might end up in jail for a different kind of flashing.

Sometimes the sooner we embrace change, the better. After makeup melting off my face enough times, I finally quit wearing any, which saved time and money. I'm grateful not having to shave my legs as often because the hair on them grows slower now. Even so, I've quit wearing shorts since a neighbor boy asked why my legs had so many cracks in them. My varicose veins *do* look a little like a road map. The time saved not shaving I now use to pluck my wildly growing facial hair.

Finding the positives makes change easier to accept. Who knows, one day I may even *embrace* change. If it doesn't involve my blanket, or old T-shirt, or . . .

Poetry – Honorable Mention
Laura L. Hansen

Laundry and Reproach
Snuggled up to my fresh-from-the-dryer clothes
the old dog waits for me
to come in and smooth his whiskers back
and scratch his chin.

The pile of clothes, laundered this morning,
now carries the taint of his doggy breath,
a near-moistness where his cold black nose
has rested.

If I move them now, set them aside
for tomorrow's folding, I will wake him
and he will sigh and lift his world-weary eyes
to me in disappointment.

They say we are perfect in the eyes of our pets,
that dogs see us as nothing but wonderful,
but my dog looks at me at times
with the eyes of a wise, hopeful teacher.

I struggle like a just-below-average student,
do my best to gain his praise, but there
are days when I fail the test, wait
too late to come home,

rise too early, forget to buy a new bag
of food and then I feel his reproach.
Still, he is a dog who easily forgives
and I am ever in need of forgiveness.

Poetry
Jan Chronister

Personal Effects

As I sort through Mother's things,
I find clean tissues tucked
in every purse and pocket.
Three hours later I have
filled a garbage sack
with discarded softness.

A summer satchel hides
a paper listing her prescriptions
extending life past ninety.

At the bottom of a box
I discover blue silk so thin
it slips to the floor. Still in the bag
are thread and buttons for a blouse
she will never make.
I see her on that day, dressed and shopping.

I reach for a square of unused
comfort and weep.

Poetry
Marsha Foss

Iron
(nautical—lying head to the wind and unable to turn either way)
No matter how strong the gust
she steered us straight.
No matter how deep the water
she anchored our boat

while the rust of sadness
ate away
bit by bit
her solid chains
and unmoving weight
until dust
was all that remained.

And we drifted away.

Poetry
Meridel Kahl

Doe

Leaving prints
of cloven perfection
in the evening's
soft snow,
she touches
my window
with her nose.

Our eyes,
hers and mine,
cradle hushed surprise
falling like a sigh
from a universe
of ancient stars

until she turns
floats through the gate
her tail
plumed white
against
ink black.

Creative Nonfiction
Audrey Kletscher Helbling

A Lot of Prairie and a Little New York

Blue veins run like rivers through the geography of my hands.

As I connect those words, I recognize the irony. I'm not good at geography. I lack in map reading skills, except on the gridded prairie. I've lived my entire life in Minnesota, never traveled west of a mile into Wyoming and only ever saw the ocean once, the Atlantic while a college junior.

Forty years ago, I crammed into a Buick with four other students—all strangers—for a Spring Break trip that landed me at an aunt and uncle's house in New Jersey. We drove for twenty-four hours, stopping only to gas up and to pee.

A tour of New York City highlighted that visit in 1977. I looked every bit the tourist with my neck craned toward skyscrapers taller than the IDS Center in downtown Minneapolis. I felt uncomfortable, still do, in topography dominated by vertical lines. Grain elevators and water towers I can handle. Clusters of tall buildings shove me into the claustrophobic category.

I've often thought about that, how growing up on a dairy and crop farm in a horizontal landscape shaped me. My hands, mottled now with brown age spots, provide visual clues. Sun painted these hands that yanked cockleburs from fields, pulled thistles in the garden, hoisted hay bales into feed bunks, pedaled bikes along gravel township roads in southwestern Minnesota.

Always the view was flat with fields extending beyond my vision, the sky stretching so high I felt insignificant. Such stark vastness created in me a vulnerability. And that vulnerability grew a writer.

I write with a sense of place culled from seventeen years of prairie life. The prairie, by the essence of its plainness, evokes an awareness of details. Decades removed from this land, I can still see plow lines of clumped black soil, smell the sweetness of freshly cut alfalfa, feel the sting of wind-driven snow, hear the rustle of corn leaves, taste the earth in well water gulped from a garden hose.

I am of the prairie—of a greening cottonwood along the fence line, of a sunset firing the sky, of a disorientating blizzard, of heat waves shimmering across a cornfield.

And I am, too, of New York, of a fifty-year-old bottle of April Showers Friction Cologne that once rested upon a chest of drawers in the pink bedroom shared with a sister. On Sunday mornings I dabbed the big city fancy perfume onto my thin wrists, masking the odor of cows and of barn. Today I swirl open the cap of that fragrance bottle with fingers connected to veins of blue rivers. I swish the inch of garish green liquid inside, remember NYC and breathe in the scent of my past—of the prairie, of the place that grew me into a writer.

Fiction
Sharon Harris

Another Person's Memories

The old house is still standing. Every year or so, when I drive by it, I think it will be gone, flattened by wind or storm or perhaps just by the strength of me wanting it gone.

I grew up here, brought up by my grandparents. I still dream of the house, still wake up sweating, sobbing, trying to run but unable to.

I left here at sixteen and went as far as I could from the Midwestern town till the ocean stopped me. I spent years trying to forget the things that happened in that house and the surrounding woods. For years I drank too much and tried nearly every drug there was, trying to forget, trying to get farther away.

There were good things in the house too. The hot, lazy days and sleeping on the porch on the summer nights. I had many pets. I went fishing. I swam in a nearby lake. I helped bring cows home from pasture, the drone of grasshoppers loud in my ears, swatting mosquitoes and deer flies. There were many chores to do, animals to care for, kittens and calves to love.

I remember the huge fields, the tall green grass murmuring in the wind, laying down on my back—seeing only sky above the waving greenness around me. I wished that was all I had to think about, to worry about, wished that everything else was gone but the summer day's heat and the sky far above me, nothing touching me but good things.

Poetry
Peter Stein

we all leave on the exhale
when you let go
     a typhoon will form in the Pacific

and soak a quarter of the world's population
     as you make landfall

this time no bullet can stop you
     from breathing in warm ocean air

sure, you'll shutter windows
     and drown out rush hour, but

you'll extend your reach inland
     to settle in a field
          that sorely misses water

Poetry
Yvonne Pearson

Morning Rain

Morning rain hangs water drops glowing with sun
on the clothesline. I shake off the glinting drops.
When Russia's Chernobyl nuclear plant melted down,
when the Fukushima plant broke open,
did their raindrops glow with radiation?
How much time does it take to heal?
I clip up tiny blue overalls, a daisy-painted skirt,
and white dress shirts, a 50/50 cotton blend.
This palette of our lives.
I have photographed so many clotheslines—
turquoise towels and jewel green dresses in Tortola,
brick red sheets and brown trousers in Bedouin backyards,
sundresses and bikinis floating on lines in Florida—
so many hopeful lives.
I clip up the lavender dress my girl wore
when we thought we'd lost her, dropped off
on the wrong side of town by the school bus driver.
We come back from these things, heal, mostly,
and there hang the blue stretch pants for her gymnastics class.
There hangs the receiving blanket for the child swelling my belly
and the flowered sheet, the one that held our wet, loving bodies
when we bet on the future,
bet against unnatural rain,
bet on the clothesline that
there would always be time enough.

Poetry
Mary Schmidt

Venom Pharm

Endlessly mending of what is torn by day
she cloaks in shadows
descends from darkened rafters
drains and devours what catches her eyes by night.

She is hardwired to avoid human contact
but it's her silk they want
for artificial ligaments, bullet-proof clothing
a provision of greater strength.

Tapping this natural resource
it's her venom they need
a medicine ideal for chronic pain
and muscular dystrophy.

No longer can she suspend by choice
to swing in the breeze of air's weave
sealed in a glass, this spider—a gift
her fangs now milked for life.

Creative Nonfiction
Kristin Laurel

Grasshopper

for Benny

One day I went for a walk and tried to be a Buddhist. This will be easy, I thought. I just need to remember, "All of life is marked by suffering and suffering is caused by desire and attachment." As I was mindfully walking down the trail, grasshoppers were jumping everywhere. I was trying hard not to step on one. But then what would it matter if I did? I wasn't supposed to be attached to anything. I wondered if the grasshopper was attached to this earth. And then I worried, maybe you had come back as a grasshopper and if I stepped on you and killed you, how would I know? If we are all connected, I am confusing everything. Busy little mind. Concentrate.

So I went back to trying to clear my head, but then I thought, "Who cares, who wouldn't have been attached to you?" Besides, you were only two and we never talked about things like this; we stayed and played in the present. I wondered if you ever got to catch a grasshopper. And I'm not sure what prayer is anymore but I chased one down and scooped him up and held it above my head and said, "This one's for you, Benny." I only held him for a few seconds as he squirmed and it tickled so I giggled. When I unclenched my fist, he flew forward and upward and I never saw him again. But I know he's still out there—in the tall grass, in the fleeting meadow.

Poetry
Charmaine Pappas Donovan

Brushstroked into Being

Many times I look in and out of a brand-new day,
see the immense beauty
my taken-for-granted eyes
translate into excruciating detail.
I can weep for joy
at the balance of light and shadow
at the perfect pictures nature makes day-in, day-out.

Brushstroked into being,
the artist's self-portrait is a short-haired woman
presenting the gift of a pine cone;
her arm becomes the branch of that Norway pine.
There are other symbols, too: grape vines
and a raptor rides her shoulder.
More painted tree parts. Her naked legs
in the foreground are strong-looking—
contoured with rippled calves.

I wish not to be her,
but to possess the arm holding the paint brush,
that arrow on her weather vane of creativity,
her flesh and blood and eye
which shape this fine woman-made vision.

Fiction – Honorable Mention
Audrey Kletscher Helbling

Art Obsession

She sorted through the art, flipping scratched frames forward to reveal generic prints by unknown artists. Fruit bowls and cute kitties, mountain landscapes and plunging waterfalls, daisies in a field and peonies drooping in a vase.

Nothing in the thrift store stock pleased her. Nora wanted art with texture and depth. Original paintings, not prints rolled off some factory line for the masses. She craved scenes painted with passion. Poetry on canvas. Hues and curves and shapes dancing across paper.

Already her art collection was sizable, bordering on obsession. She shopped garage sales and second-hand stores, seeking cast-offs and unappreciated art. She grabbed Myrtle's rendering of gladioli, the petals thick with oil paint. For $5 she snagged a framed Harvey Dunn giclee. The homestead scene of a pioneer woman gathering prairie flowers inspired her to appreciate even the plainest of landscapes.

Nora was drawn to the everyday, and to the exotic in a dark-skinned girl painted on burlap by Mexican folk artist Jose Maria de Servin. Only after she purchased a piece did she research the artist. She bought with her soul, not with a desire to acquire art for its monetary value.

Jimmy didn't understand. He questioned the sensibility of such spending. She tried to explain that the absence of art during her childhood created this need to surround herself with it. She needed pastoral scenes of grazing cows, sweeps of waves caressing a beach, a handsome couple dancing the tango.

After a while, Jimmy stopped questioning. Not that it mattered. Nora continued filing through thrift store donations and household excess. One Saturday morning in mid-June, she thrilled in the discovery of familiar paint-by-number ballerina portraits. Tutus flared in shades of blue. Haunting brown eyes connected with Nora. She remembered brushing paint across coded numbers printed on cardboard. And she remembered, too, the day her father destroyed her ballerina paintings.

"There will be no dancing in this house," he said.

Poetry
Sharon Chmielarz

Her Desire to Change
from Green into Yellow
or: Death as Dandelion

Her crown
on one day
turns ghostly,
a worn halo.
What used
to be.

A strong wind
gusts around
and then that, too,
—the ghost of her
—is gone.

to reappear—
(given a full
amount of time)
as vision.

She is!
Dandelions,
everywhere!

Poetry
Deborah Rasmussen

Alaska Morning
We position ourselves on deck,
an eager audience
before Margerie Glacier
which glows turquoise today
against a pewter sea.

We hope to see it calve,
drop its offspring into the ocean
spawning waves
that will rock our boat
like a cradle
in this nursery of ice.

When it happens
we proclaim the wonder,
the magnificence,
the power,
the unbearable beauty
while all around us
nature carries on

unaware.

Poetry
Marsha Foss

landscape with lake cabin on a hill and a few sad notes at night

From the beach
I hear mandolin,
harmonica, flute,
laughter of dear friends.
Old songs
make the night seem
cloudless. It is not.

On the dock my dangling feet
touch cold lake water
splashing the surface
in sync with sounds
of merry, then melancholy, music
from the cabin above.

A loon surfaces.
Quietly we call
into the dark and
stark starless expanse
of sky,
of lake.

Like the lonely loon
I listen for an answer.
Hearing none, we dive
into the deep and murky water.
Cloudless it is not.
Cloudless it is not.

Creative Nonfiction
Sharon Harris

Give Him Some Credit

"Your ma died last night, kids. She's been really sick. She's gone." So spoke Pa, his eyes wet. The three kids, five and seven and nine, huddled together in bewilderment. It was 1921 and their mother had just died of pneumonia. *Gone? Gone where? Was she lost?* Not understanding, they went outside and searched for her.

This slant of sun, this piece of sky, this house and barn and yard—the place that had always been their home now felt strange. Would tomorrow even come? The world they had known had disappeared with Pa's words. They used to feel safe but now nothing felt the same. Their world had failed them and tilted beneath their feet.

The neighbors talked about his drinking. But give him credit. He stayed with the children. He ran the farm, he sold the milk and vegetables, hauling them in the wagon pulled by their two horses, driving away with the jingle of harness and the clomp of big hooves. As the days passed, he milked the cows, he planted the fields, he butchered a pig when he needed to.

It was a harsh life. The children had to do chores they shouldn't have to do. They tried to learn to cook and wash clothes and help with the livestock. But they had no one to run to for hugs. Their father had no time for that. But give him credit. He did stay.

Often he drank so he could forget her face, her bright smile, the hope and the plans in her eyes. Nearly every night, he drove his horses and wagon to town to buy beer and drink to forget.

And nearly every night, the three children stood out at the end of the driveway in the dark. They were waiting with no supper, listening for the jingle of harness and the thump of horses' hooves, wondering if Pa was coming home.

Poetry
Tarah L. Wolff

The Old Farmer

His pickup is parked on the side of the highway
held together by rust, duct tape and wire
a testament to American engineering
he is too
On this hot morning
I can see him through the heat waving up
off the black top (on my way to work)
His silhouette includes the oldest John Deere
baseball cap that is
still being worn and the ever practical short-sleeved
cotton shirt
He seems ancient (as the rest of us fly past)
head bowed over
his dog laid out at his feet, neither one of them
moving at all

Creative Nonfiction
Audrey Kletscher Helbling

The Weekly Phone Call

It's 6:30 p.m. on Sunday when I punch the green phone icon.

"Hello, Arlene speaking," she answers, the indiscernible dialogue of a television blaring in the background.

"Hi, this is Audrey," I say, then wait while she turns off her TV. "How are you doing?"

Her answer never deviates. She is tired and blames the weather. Already sadness threads through my thoughts. Inside the sheltered walls of a care center, she can't feel the bite of a winter prairie wind, the drench of rainfall, the smothering humidity of a July afternoon. She feels only artificial heat and cold while sequestered in her over-sized dorm-style room.

My mind drifts as Mom laments an in-house obsession with Bingo, recounts an escape attempt by a friend—big and exciting news—and complains of failed jets in the whirlpool tub. I listen, insert appropriate responses, and await the usual repetition of information.

When she repeats herself, I say nothing. There is no point. My love prevails in silence. But inside, my anger rises at her declining memory. I want the mom who never forgot a birthday, who remembered what she ate for lunch, who knew names. I miss her undeniably kind and positive spirit. I am grieving.

But I tell her none of this. Instead, I end our conversation with "I love you" and a promise to call her next Sunday, at 6:30 p.m.

Poetry
René Bartlett Montgomery

Kitchen Stories

Look in the kitchens,
discover the ways
people left their marks:
precise stitches
that mend frayed towels,
wooden spoons
wearing varied burns, once
placed too close to flames
during a busy meal.
Leftover spoons,
lost salt shakers,
marks on the wall—
all stories of origins:
stories of laughing,
of planning,
of recreating the same
chicken and dumplings,
or chili, or pot pies
year after year,
generation after generation.
Martyrs revealed
in ordinary deeds,
signs of those now
resting from their labors.
Hold them close,
feel the love they breathed.

Fiction
Carol Dunbar

The Red Coat

All month Luvera has been up here in the attic sorting through old clothes for the church sale, and it had surprised her when Hester's mother asked for a party. She knew how hard it was for her to ask for anything, but they could all use one, to cheer everybody up. Hester turning eight. The party at six. Luvera with her one present.

She holds up the coat. Just touching it brings it all back. How the scarlet wool had called to her from across the fabric store, the pattern next to it on display, all of it so reminiscent of her childhood, an earlier time, the innocence of it, and she had felt charged with this desire to make the perfect coat—it just overtook her. Still it surprises her to see how well constructed it is because she had no idea what she was doing at the time, but all these years it's held up. The heavy wool, the hood with its vanilla fleece lining, wooden button closures and cuffed sleeves. She hasn't made anything like it since, couldn't repeat this again if she wanted to, and what's more it was made not for an infant but for a young girl. So who else could it be for? God must have known all along. *Do not lay up your treasures where moths and rust consume.*

From downstairs the dog barks and her husband's voice, always so good with the children, followed the sound of their little footsteps in their great big old house.

"Aunt Luvera, can I come up? I have a surprise for you."

She can't move. Loss doesn't soften over time; it gets wider and deeper like a lake. You get used to it being there, to going around it, but sometimes you just fall in.

"Aunt Luvera?" Her little face appears in the attic floor, at the opening where the wooden stairs pull down.

"It's all right. You can come up."

The girl climbs the last few steps up into the attic with her clunky boots, wearing a homespun sweater fastened one button hole off so that the pocket hangs down lopsided on one side.

"Aunt Luvera? I made this for you." She holds out a little ghost on a stick, the sheet cinched with orange yarn over a popcorn ball, eyes drawn with marker. She chose brown marker, not the color of her own eyes, but once the color of her father's eyes.

Hester goes still. "Aunt Luvera? Are you crying?"

"You never saw me cry before?"

She shakes her head, *No*.

"Is it cold out?"

She nods.

"Windy?"

"Not too bad. Just a little nippy."

Just a little nippy. Where do they learn to say things like that?

Hester fiddles with her ghost on a stick. "Why are you sad?"

If anyone could understand it would be this child. So, it just comes out of her.

"I thought your uncle and I would have our own family by now, but I had a baby and she died. Her name was Katie. She would be fifteen now if she had lived, but she was born too early, and there were abnormalities, and so she died. I was too afraid after that to try again."

Hester goes to her and wraps her in a hug. She holds her so tight, and they console one another in the dusty purple light. They talk to each another in high whispered voices close to each other's ears, soft sounds that no one else can hear. After enough time has passed, Luvera wipes her eyes and sets aside the little ghost on its stick.

"Now I have something for you." She picks up the coat. "I was going to wrap this for your birthday but you might as well have it now. It's going to snow."

Hester's eyes brim.

"Go ahead." Luvera holds it out. "Well now, look at that. Fits you perfectly." She adjusts the collar, tugs at the sleeves.

Hester lifts the hood and turns. For a moment only the side

of her cheek is visible, and there is the instant, the barest of seconds in which Luvera has a glimpse of the way it could have been: her own daughter, putting on her coat on an ordinary day. Her own daughter standing there. *I'm going outside, Mama. Back in a jiffy.*

Back in a jiffy. Where do they learn to say things like that?

Poetry
Peggy Trojan

Art
The simple drawing
on the rough cave wall
done thousands
of years ago
is still vital.
What is important
does not need detail.
Only a few lines
of recognition.
Only awareness.

Poetry
Janice Larson Braun

Puppy Love

Brutus has grown old—
Warm, chocolate eyes
Have become muddy,
His shiny black coat
Now coarse and grizzled.

I reach into the backseat
Of the pickup where he sits
To stroke his cheek.

He melts
Into my caress
And closes his eyes
When I lean in to kiss
His forehead.

Poetry
Marlys Guimaraes

Dining with Scott Kelly

He, with his beef stew flattened into a square pouch
and I, with cheese-covered bread, toasted to a light brown.

He warms his in a space station suitcase for twenty minutes.
My Cuisinart toaster takes exactly 1.5 minutes.

No microwave? I wonder, as he pushes a button to
fill a pouch of dehydrated asparagus with hot water, then
                    waits . . .

My tea is served in a fine china teacup, pink with gold edges.
His plastic pouch of lemonade, which he says is "a little too
                    sweet,"

is rehydrated with water brought in from supply shuttles or
reprocessed urine. He reports that the urine water is clear

and better tasting than water shuttled in. His dining room doesn't
                    have
an Ashley dining set like mine, or even a chair, but rather a metal
                    counter

the size of four placemats. He stands, spoons, and catches flying
                    food
into his mouth while NBC nightly news, beamed from earth,
                    blares and

bounces off equipment-filled walls. A Russian floats by,
                    untethered.
"A year is a long time," I think, sipping my non-urinated tea in
                    silence.

Poetry
Florence Witkop

Hubble

A slow, sweet curve of light
Heads out towards infinity,
Serenely passing galaxies
Of brand new planets spitting fire
And old ones wrapped in ice.
Undying, awesome, blindingly pristine
Unseen
Unheard
Unknown
Untouched
Unfelt
Until,
It recklessly
Collides with me
And, dying,
Tells me all it knows
Of space and time and life.

Poetry
Charles Johnson

Jimmy Gets an Earful

You know, someday, Jimmy, I'm just gonna get my big fat butt
outa this big fat rut in this sad-sack dinky town, never minding
where I go and get in the ol' Chevy, start it up like I always do,
put it in gear almost even before it starts and take off for places
'way down the road—like, oh geez, I don't know, way so far away
that I'll change time zones two, three times before I really stop
since I've never done this kinda thing before—treat myself to a
night in a fancy schmancy top notch hotel with an all-night diner
and I can sit there till after one in the morning eatin' fried pork
chops that come with a slog o' steamed vegetables and a big
mushy pile o' mashed potatoes swimmin' in the greasiest kind o'
gravy that slabbers down my chin—greasy enough that I need to
clean it off with an extra napkin or two from Penny the waitress,
who, by the way, Jimmy, will catch your eye 'cuz she's so pretty
and so perky that she'll be worth puttin' on my best flirtin' moves
jes' to see how she acts and I'll finish that meal with a dessert like
I never get at home, ordering it with extra coconut and whipped
cream (like Gramma always used to ask, "Have a little dessert
with your whipped cream?") and Penny will say in her sweet
voice, "Ah come on, you don't havta tip me that much" but I do it
anyway when I pay my tab—so I go to my room with one of
those vibrating dealies in the bed where you put in a quarter that
makes you relax and fall asleep just-like-that, making me dream
I'm a cowboy in an old black-and-white western on TV where
everybody in the wagon train loves me, even the little kids,
because I have a fast draw and can shoot straight pretty much all
the time and I saved the preacher's wife from falling over the cliff
and so on like that until I wake up—and then, Jimmy, and only
then will I consider coming back here and have things get back to
normal where I go to work every day, come home at night and
kick off my shoes but you can know for sure I was glad I went
and did all that stuff and would do it again if I thought I needed
to.

Poetry
Joni Norby

Bees
buzz and bob
inside my head—
no concern for the
dread bred from
the threat of
their never-ending
menace.
They rub antennae
with pollen-snouted
bees now bumbling about
my potting shelf.
Together they dabble
and dab until life
bursts through
budding bulbs
sprung from this weary
perennial heart.

Creative Nonfiction
Bonnie West

I love Technology

In 1968 I heard the red-eyed computer, HAL, say *I'm sorry, Dave. I'm afraid I can't do that* while refusing to open the pod doors, and I was never the same.

I knew computers would change the world. For Dave and the crew it wasn't a good change, but I saw then how magnificent it was going to be. I left the theater imagining a computer that could someday talk to you and help you navigate through life. I dreamed of the telephones which might exist, like those in the film where you could actually *see* the person you were talking to from as far away as a space station on the moon.

Thirty-three years later, when 2001 rolled around for real, computers had gone way beyond the *Space Odyssey*. And by 2015 the abilities of our first computers, those that once filled a room the size of an airplane hanger, were laughable next to computers we held in our hands. Most delightful to me, my computer-phone could not only make a video call, it could indeed, talk.

Siri?

Yes, Bonnie?

Face-time my grandsons, please.

Just to confirm, you'd like to face-time your grandsons?

Yes, thank you, Siri.

Don't mention it.

And there they are running around their Swedish apartment.

This technology not only amazes me, it frees me from loneliness. It allows me to long, not quite so desperately, for my daughter overseas and my son in Alaska. And if I'm concerned or have a funny thought, my children are available, instantly texting answers.

For entertainment I can always turn on the phone and say, *What is the meaning of life, Siri?* And Siri might reply, *I can't answer that now, but give me some time to write a very long play in which nothing happens.*

And now I am a senior. I loved being a senior in high school launching myself confidently into an unknown future but now, not so much. My impending launch is more predictable and I'm less excited. I am however, a realist, and understand with age comes inevitable faltering and, eventually, the possibility of having to live alongside strangers. But now, because of technology, I'll have much greater freedom. Likely, I'll have my own red-eyed HAL blinking in my living room and rather than destroy me it will protect me, check my vitals, remind me to turn off the stove, and allow me to live not only for a longer time alone but, also, unafraid,

Still, the time will come when, even with the help of a computer, I'll be incapable on my own. Technology is advancing exponentially and I'm counting on being housed somewhere, fed somehow, and outfitted internally with a virtual reality chip which will send me into an alternate universe where I will feel as though I'm hiking the Scottish Highlands, sailing the Baltic, reading Chekov, listening to Mahler and perhaps, if I'm very, very lucky, phoning home from a space station on the moon.

Ryan M. Neely
Creative Nonfiction

Agendas

My grandmother died. It's a simple statement. Elegant.
My grandmother died.

After heavy rain deep in the forest when the fragrance of leaves and moss and lichen reaches up to greet you, sometimes it carries with it the fragrance of decay. Death. Just a hint. Nothing tangible. Nothing to grab onto, to analyze. Nothing of which to be conscious.

It was the same with my memories of her.

The other grandkids—my cousins—they sat in a circle on the floor before the funeral and told stories of Grandma teaching them to drive, of her filming us lip-syncing Michael Jackson, of the craft drawers she kept in her house. At best, my memories range as far back as the last time I saw her alive, stuck in that stupid chair, withering away, unable to recognize even her own husband.

Grandpa sat alone during the visitation. Isolated. Wrapped in a cloak of his faith and prayer. He hoped God would comfort him, but each time he stood to greet another mourner he clenched his hands behind his back to keep others from seeing him shake.

It's not like you can ask him what he's been up to. Seven hundred days spent at her bedside while CNAs and Hospice Nurses flitted in and out, what could he say? "You know. Waiting for Grandma to die." And you can't ask him what his plans are now, like it's some kind of graduation leading into the rest of his life. But you want to, you want to remind him his own life isn't over, that he shouldn't give up, but already you see the shadow of death lingering behind him.

Aunt Julie had to make sure the casket wasn't displayed

under the kids' drawings from Sunday School. "It just seems tacky." And Uncle David argued against any kind of embalming because "those chemicals aren't good for the environment," and the pastor felt it a perfect opportunity for a recruitment speech. "If you haven't enlisted for Christ, better hurry so you can see Dorothy again."

It's all morbid. Narcissistic. You spend thousands of dollars to preserve a shell, a set of clothes so you can parade it around, congregate with others, stare at it, talk to it like there's still a person there, before you shove it in the ground never to be seen again. You bawl over it, not because you're sad for it, like it's somehow worse off than it was before. You cry for yourself. You cry over a lost possession, something you'll never have again like a child who dropped its favorite toy out the car window on the Interstate.

Relax.

Take a breath.

My grandmother died, but the sun will rise tomorrow and the world goes on.

Poetry
Peggy Trojan

Home
I know what it is
to weep in the night
wanting to give up
and go home
knowing I can't
because
I'm already there.

Poetry
Olivia Anderson

Heritage

Aspens are turning the same color your eyelashes would in October sunrise and fall; they fall gold as we watch. Quietly sandhill crane becomes target, annoyance evident—they are the reason for our lack of corn. Birds chirp harmonious, deer tracks mark up the fields like poplars beside creaking windmill. I hear myself in Grandpa's "Oh, sure," Grandma's "You betcha," breathed out visibly now, cold. Leaves are still falling, mixing with voices. Car doors open, slam, gravel crunches with frost.

Creative Nonfiction – Honorable Mention
Janet Kurtz

Pressing Matters

"What are you doing crawling across the top of the bed?" I asked my ninety-year-old mother as she pulled the sheet toward the opposite side. "It's a tight squeeze, but you can walk around the edge."

"I'm lining up the stripes," she replied. "It's really easy with this pattern to just line them up."

"Why do they need to be lined up?" I asked, perplexed.

"So that I can sleep better at night."

"But, your eyes will be shut," I pointed out while leaning over to help line up the last set of stripes on my side.

"True. But, I will know." She smiled sweetly.

"Is this like your habit of hanging up clothes by color and size?"

She patted down the bedspread, crawled back across and slid off the bed as she explained.

"It's artistic. I love to hang up clothes. Our condo ought to allow clotheslines. Why, kids these days don't even know the smell of freshly aired laundry!" She bemoaned yet another loss to the most recent generation born on earth.

"Well, I guess they'll never know the love of ironing, either," I added. "Remember the time you ironed my underpants? Sheets maybe, but underwear?"

She threw me a pseudo-scowl. "I like to iron. Besides having stripes lined up, I like to sleep on ironed sheets. And, I like them to fit. Not like the queen-sized ones on my regular bed at home. It's such a struggle to tuck them in, but at least they don't wrinkle. You see, I have cut back on ironing," she said as if vindicated.

"Okay, you're improving," I conceded. "But how about the habit of counting things? Remember the time you counted all the paddle strokes when we canoed back from Virgin Lake to Julia?"

"It's uninhabited wilderness. I did it to pass the time," she said, then added, "plus, I wanted to know."

"But, Mom, you counted for one and a half hours," I protested. "I was enjoying the white lilies, turtles, eagles and—"

"That was a long time ago," she interrupted.

I laughed, unconvinced.

"Hey, Mom," I said, changing the subject. "How about we go berry picking? Maybe we'll find enough for breakfast." I grabbed two berry boxes. "Ya coming?"

Walking along the lane, we spied some raspberry bushes and plucked a few remaining tiny berries. The pickings were slim.

She peered into my box and squealed, "That's not okay! You have more than I do!"

"We could count them," I offered with a grin.

"Exactly what I was thinking," she smirked. "How 'bout we just put them together and go fix breakfast?"

At breakfast, she placed two dishes of berries on the table.

"There," she said. "I combined them."

"Good job, Mom," I said. "Now, we'll both get our fair share."

"Of course, we will. I counted them."

Poetry
Richard G. Hagen

Lilies
after seeing a pencil sketch
fine lines
remind me to go
to my garden to
invest silent time
slowly seeing the lilies

intense color   fragility
vigorous impermanence

in winter there will be only
fine lines

Poetry
Renee Loehr

Outdoor Cuisine

Rooftops frosted
with frothy white icing.

Snow banks carved
like loaves of bread.

Gateposts topped with
scoops of vanilla ice cream.

Mounds of mashed potatoes
peppered with dirt.

Cream whipped to a frenzy
piled high by ferocious winds.

An inedible menu
of winter fare.

Fiction
Marcia Neely

Transplant Day

The phone rang at 2:38 a.m. on December 20. Only a moment passed between the ring and answer. Thoughts flashed through my mind to the beat of my racing heart. *Middle of the night—JW's in the hospital—Has he died?—Is he dying?—Where's Misty?—Was Greg in an accident?*

I heard, "We have a donor."

Within minutes John and I were on our way to Abbott Northwestern Hospital where a nurse was awakening our sixteen-year-old son JW to prepare him for heart-double lung transplantation. Snow fell; a fierce north wind created swirls of white.

While John and I headed toward the hospital, "at some god-awful hour," JW would tell us later, "I heard a voice, 'JW, JW.'"

"We have a donor," said Transplant Coordinator Nancy Siemers.

"There was a feeling as in a dream where you're falling. You wake up just before you hit the ground," remembered JW. "Then I became numb. I was scared. You and Dad weren't there. I began to cry. I was afraid you wouldn't make it. I began shaking.

"Then I got up and began routines. I painted myself with Betadine, brushed my teeth and washed my face. I thought the way I was acting was weird, that I shouldn't be acting normal.

"I became afraid again, thinking that being wheeled into surgery might be the last thing I ever remembered, that I wouldn't see you again."

At 5:40, John and I pulled into the parking lot at Abbott Northwestern Hospital. I hopped out of the car and ran toward the hospital entrance. Out of breath, I told the receptionist that our son was having a heart-lung transplant. "Where will we find him?"

The receptionist directed us to the surgery unit in the basement. It was quiet there. Dark. John and I raced back to the receptionist. We learned JW was still in his room on Station 41.

He had a smile on his face when we walked into room 4150. "It looks like you're getting your Christmas wish," I said. JW began to cry.

"I'm excited. I'm scared. I'm being given an opportunity to live; someone else is dead or dying," he whimpered.

A nurse transferred JW to a gurney, wheeled him to a room outside the surgery unit. Nurses prepared him for the operation while I gently rubbed his face. After a nurse gave him a pubic shave, he quipped, "I'm sort of like Dad now. I have a prematurely bald head."

Mildly sedated, JW softly wept much of the time.

John gave a thumbs-up sign when a nurse wheeled JW toward the operating room. Just before the OR door closed, I saw JW's thumbs high in the air.

It was time to wait. Hope. Sitting in the surgery waiting room, I sighed, sighed again. I read JW's horoscope for December 20, printed in the Minneapolis StarTribune: "You will receive a priceless gift from someone you have helped in the past."

Creative Nonfiction
Georgia A. Greeley

The Yucca

Right before going to bed, my husband knocked it over and left it; the baby Yucca lay there, bare-rooted, breathing night air, no dirt, no moisture, just it's three light-green prickly fingers and worm-like roots panting in the dark. Waiting. I got out of bed the next morning as soon as he told me, carefully lifted the tender plant, gathered the spilled dirt back into the pot, pushed a hole into the loosened soil, and gently set the roots in the finger-sized hole, sprinkling the last of the recovered dirt over those dusty white roots. I didn't tamp the dirt down and bruise the tissue. I let the water I drizzled into the pot refresh the Yucca and swirl the dirt snugly around the rootlets. This plant is still vulnerable. No living thing can be left naked for hours in the dark without repercussions.

Poetry
Richard G. Hagen

An Etheree

He
couldn't
care less for
spring's magical
scents colorfully
bursting, wildly, with life
so energetically.
He was an old mortician who
too long breathed air fragrant only with for-
meldahyde. Only his memories blossom.

Creative Nonfiction – Honorable Mention
Sue Bruns

Waiting

We sit in silence on the kitchen floor, our backs against the cupboard doors, waiting for the ambulance. I pull him toward me so he doesn't collapse sideways and hit his head. The tile floor is sticky with the morphine and medicine that spilled when we tried to inject it into his feeding tube. We sit and stare blindly ahead.

"They'll be here soon," I say.

He has completed five of the seven weeks of treatment—radiation and chemo. Last Friday's double dose of radiation zapped his energy. He spent most of the weekend in the recliner, sleeping heavily. On Sunday, he declined my invitation to go for a walk with the dogs and, later that evening, when he got up from the chair, he lost his balance. I heard the crash from the kitchen as he fell forward, tried to catch himself on the end table as it slid across the floor and broke his fall.

I ran out. "Are you okay?"

He was lifting himself up. He nodded.

On Monday he'd lost his balance again and had fallen to the ground, catching himself once again. This morning after radiation he had a slight fever. By the time we checked into oncology, it was 100.7.

"No chemo today," the doctor said. "We'll give you some fluids and I'll prescribe some antibiotics."

As he sat in the chair, the fluid sack hanging over his right shoulder, drip, drip, dripping into his IV, he couldn't stay awake. Even when we played cribbage, he dozed between plays of the cards. When the bag was empty, the nurse removed the IV. I helped him put on his coat and cap. He stumbled as he walked away from the chair.

"Whoa," said the nurse, reaching for his elbow. She and I exchanged a look. "I'll walk you to the car," she said. I was glad she did. He wouldn't question her doing this but, yesterday, when I had reached for him as he tottered, he'd pulled away, brushing me off. I understood. He didn't want help. He wanted to do things on his own.

But now he has no choice but to accept help. If I could get him into the car by myself and drive him to the ER, I would, but he can't get up. His legs are like rubber. He stares at them as if they've betrayed him. Minutes ago, when he tried to crawl into the living room to get into his chair, his arms betrayed him, too. He wobbled as he tried to get them to move before he gave up.

His eyes are unfocused, half-shut, his head heavy. It carries his upper body forward, and I reach over to push him back against the cupboard.

He starts to doze again and I am left alone to wonder: how much worse can this get?

Poetry
Kathryn Knudson

New York Pizza

During our vacation the only question he
asked me was if we could go for real pizza,

as he called it. Slice of pepperoni sprinkled
with garlic, Parmesan, and pepper flakes,

then folded over.
It's the water, apparently.

The only thing he wanted was to lean against
a counter next to dripping umbrellas, sneaking

a slice before dinner with my college friends.
To me it tasted like any other thin crust pizza.

Nothing more.
So, yeah, I think that's when I knew.

Poetry
Lane Rosenthal

Without You
The dispassionate moon
swims in an amber-ringed
milky pool
reflecting life without you:
silvery cold,
a hint of color at the edges.
Wisps of clouds
glide like memories
across that implacable face
and tears drop
   one by one
      like dying stars.

Poetry
Tarah L. Wolff

Barefoot

I tip-toe down
to the killing floor
loathe to wake him and
see the wounds I
inflicted the night
before

There is no more silent a place
than the gallows afterward
when the boards have been
swept clean and the
audience has taken the last
living image
home with them

Stepping out on our deck
I imagine they applauded

Poetry
Cheryl Weibye Wilke

Mexican Music

at the beach. At first
they turned it up to rival
the volume and speed
of conversation between sons

and brothers, sisters and
wives. Grandfather wearing
a white straw hat
sat quiet at the southeast

harbor of the lawn chair circle, relaxed
in the shade. And then they noticed
me and turned the music down
like fearing a crack

in an iron anchor. Someone
then turned it up. And
the conversation resumed.
A child pouted from the center

of attention. Threads of intimate
humor teased to untie bowline knots
into unfettered laughter. I'm glad.
I like their songs of brown eyes

crooning and foot-stomping Spanish—
rolling ruffles of cotton
white, green, and red. Music
wafting of margaritas and

splashes of lime. I don't
understand a word, but the banter waxes
and wanes like the warm, rippling
waves of this sultry mid-summer. I long

to wash up upon their shore.

Creative Nonfiction
René Bartlett Montgomery

Fear of Flying Cockroaches

"There are flying cockroaches there." My sister's lips curled up in a jealous, devious smile. I can handle a bug or two. I grew up camping with a father who worked as the science specialist at boy scout camps. I had my limits, though.

Now, I stood near the freezer of a small market near the school in Japan where I taught English. Since arriving, my food consisted of meager pickings from the convenience store in my building. Hunger forced me into this market. I stood concentrating on the packaging, trying to find something recognizable. I thought I discovered a pizza, but instead of pepperoni, it was squid, seaweed, and corn that covered the top. I look out to check if Katsuyo, my Japanese colleague, had arrived. She promised to help me find food to fill my little pink refrigerator. I turned back into the store and discovered a display of blue and white cans. *Pocari Sweat?* I giggled. *What is a Pocari, and who wants to drink its sweat?* I looked for more desirable goods.

I couldn't speak or read Japanese, which made my task more difficult. Many labels contained English words, but they served only popular appeal and seemed ridiculous. For example, a box of candy boasted: "Find great pleasure sucking sweet hard balls." I laughed, knowing the fun *SNL* could have with that.

As I became anxious waiting for Katsuyo, I felt a soft movement on my hair. I had not yet seen the flying cockroaches my sister warned of but, based on the insects I had seen, I feared the worst. My blood-curling screams would empty the market—if not the town. I willed my mind not to picture a giant flying bug in my hair, and felt a firmer tug on my tresses. Before I turned around, I heard Katsuyo speaking in Japanese. As I turned, I saw

175

an adorable, small, old woman dressed in a plain blue kimono with a pink obi. I had seen girls in formal kimonos with faces painted, and hair pulled in tight buns. This woman's face wore no make-up, and a simple loose ponytail held her long gray hair. Her eyes danced as she talked with Katsuyo and stole quick glances at me.

Finally, the old woman bowed to me and slowly walked away. Katsuyo explained that the woman apologized for touching my hair. She had followed me around the freezer for a while before Katsuyo arrived. The old woman came to town only a few times a year from a village in the hill country. She told Katsuyo that even though she recently celebrated her 93rd birthday, she had never seen blonde or curly hair before. I happily gave that old woman a lifetime first experience, and probably owed her more—especially since, in my eyes, she just may have saved me from my first giant flying cockroach.

Poetry
Stephanie Brown

Sunday Worship

I kneel
on a yellow pad
in my own Eden
where weeds invade
patches of dirt
not overwhelmed
by coneflowers or scarlet
bee balm.
It is here I pray
near the peonies,
heads bowed heavy,
as robins nearby devour
earthworms
with fervor and determination.

How can there be such distance
between salvation
and the tangibility of dirt?
The sermon
of the Pileated Woodpecker
drums as he moves
from dead birch to oak stump
confused, as I am,
about where to land.

Poetry
Ruth Schmidt-Baeumler

Twenty to Four
and Orion's three-star studded belt
makes its way over the tree tops.

After three foggy nights the
sky is finally clear

and the shrinking moon sickle
illuminates the surroundings.

Nothing is important barring
this beauty.

The child has already slipped
under the beltline of its mother.

We loosen the belt of our love in order
to make room for it.

There are more notches
in the belt to open,

as many as stars in the sky.

Fiction
Larry Ellingson

The Road to Ramadi

The grass is crunchy dry. If I lie on the ground I know it will be hard and prickly. This is no place for a picnic . . . a trap, a picnic-ambush? My wife is already there sitting on a blanket and she's opening the cooler. She looks up at me. I love it when she smiles; the whole of her face engages, the corners of her eyes turn down as her mouth turns up, beautiful. Instead of smiling she reaches into the cooler and hands me a soda. "How was counseling today?"

"Same old shit," I say

"You didn't go, did you?"

"No . . . but it's always the same old shit." I laugh and it fades.

She looks at me and I look back and her eyes slide away from mine.

"Look, I tried to go, I started to go, but I couldn't open the door. There are too many people; things are moving too fast." My wife is a social person, she likes being around people. She's never been afraid of people, believes she is safe.

We are in Anbar province, on a road to Ramadi. My buddy Dane is driving. Dane's wife sent him their kid's teething ring. It's shaped like an ear of corn and there are teeth marks where his kid chewed on it. Dane tied a string to it and it hangs in the Humvee. We're going down this road and the dust is flying behind us and his kid's teether is swinging back and forth, back and forth, keeping perfect time, tick, tock.

"Isn't that what the counseling is for?" she says. "We've been through this before, Pete. I can't live with you when you're like this. You're angry all the time; you take it out on me, on your friends. We're not the enemy."

Me and Dane are checking out the people we pass on the road. You never know who the bad guys are; anything is possible. An entire squad was wiped out last week, car bomb. There have been reports of IEDs buried along this road. A black car passes us, covered with dust. A bearded old man stands next to the road. He smokes and watches us as we pass. A man in a white robe and a braided headband leads a camel alongside the road. Dane points at him. Look at that, Pete, *he says,* that's something a prophet might have seen two thousand years ago and here we are, how many wars later? Why are we here again? Someone told a lie, *I say.* Here's what's true, *Dane says, snatching the teether, big grin on his face. Dane has gotten philosophical since he became a dad. We drive on.*

My hands tuck into my armpits, holsters. How can I explain? Survivor's guilt, the counselor calls it. Rage, remorse, I'm all those things. Does she expect me to come home and just flip a switch, here I am, honey, ready to live a normal life?

A cloud of sand blows across the road and when it clears we see a traffic control point ahead. The black car that passed us has pulled over to the left shoulder. We are coming up on it fast, then we're alongside the car and I feel things speeding up, a tingling runs, bang, up my spine, electric fear, a warning, a second too late.

Did I shout something? I knew something was wrong. I should have told Dane to stop, should have shouted at him to stop. I should have been driving the Humvee; it was my turn to drive, wasn't it? I need to call Dane's wife and see how they're doing. Christ, I should have done that a long time ago. Look at the young couple walking their designer dog. Got their walking-through-the-park clothes on. The guy looks upset. At the dog? At his wife? What the hell does he have to be upset about? All these people rushing around, posing, getting upset about little things. Think that they know what is real, what is true. They don't know what's going on here, buried mines, hidden bombs, lies. Maybe I need to warn them so that we can put a stop to it. If I don't warn them, it will happen again, we'll just keep going down that road, down that prophet's road.

My wife is looking at me. She opens her mouth to speak. A cool shiver creeps up my back. Tick, tock.

Poetry – Honorable Mention
James Bettendorf

The Last Battle

In a black limousine, the family whose soldier
made it back from the war that ended years ago

waits out the rain at the cemetery. The soldier
fought battles in the mind and seemed to adjust.

Her life had gone on though she struggled with thunder,
door slams, and shouts, and with shadows

that didn't announce themselves before they appeared
around corners of low buildings. She struggled

with smells—dry sand, cordite, rotting garbage.
She was devoted to and protective of her two children, born

before she left on her first tour. Respectful to strangers.
Friendly to people she knew. Her husband

feared her dreams when she screamed and flailed.
She found peace hunting alone in the forest

though she never came back with game, and her rifle
was always oiled and cleaned before she locked it

in the gun case, ready for the next hunt.
Could they have hidden the key?

Poetry
Justin Watkins

Dragging a Deer Through New Snow

The wooded sideslope
A stark monochrome
Angular blacks
A blanket of white

The hunter between these
At careful progress
Downhill toward the ravine
Bare hands on antler

A pause for rest
His breath before him
And uphill the crimson trail made
The only curve and color

Creative Nonfiction
Mary A. Conrad

Freedom vs. Fear

The fluorescent lights are on. Beige and burgundy stackable chairs surround gray tables centered in the room. A handout and pencil mark each place. Another Fearbusting Workshop is about to begin.

A dozen participants file down the hall to join me in the library. We meet here every Wednesday to share stories from the past week. Most have been here before. A few newcomers may show up; an equal number might drop out. They attend as they choose or as their schedules permit. Building rapport and maintaining this safe space is my challenge.

I welcome the group, noting familiar faces and registering new ones. I smile and say, "Hi, I'm Mary." They reply with a friendly, "Hi, Mary." They introduce themselves by their first names and greet everyone else too. Making eye contact and calling each other by name becomes a simple and comforting weekly ritual. They are used to being called by their last names, often without a smile.

We discuss how temporary dislocation from their ordinary lives creates stress and triggers fears about their future. Some are glad to be away from home. Many confess they feel safer here. Others think they might not be alive if they hadn't ended up here.

The handout suggests that seeing past experiences through a different lens changes how we view our present circumstances, opening us to new possibilities. I mention the popular Apple computer ad in the 1980s picturing Einstein with the caption "Think Different." I am surprised several remember it. They don't look old enough. I tell them Einstein once said, "We cannot solve our problems at the same level of thinking that created them."

This group likes stories about replacing negative thinking with positive thoughts. Several think they can see how this principle of inner freedom works: a traffic arrest that becomes a life-saving wake-up call; a distressing breakup that exposes an abusive domestic relationship; aggression that reveals the bitterness of unresolved resentments. They agree that lessons learned *after the fact* must be applied *in advance* the next time.

The hour goes by fast. I look at the two gray walls lined with bookshelves. Posters on another wall warn participants about inappropriate interactions with each other and me. Several empty chairs remind me that some didn't come today. A large institutional clock confirms this training is almost over. My eyes scan the circle of faces, their attention focused on me now. I smile and thank them for coming. They smile back and say, "Thanks for being here." We stand and join hands in solidarity, repeating our closing affirmation—words from Rev. Dr. Martin Luther King Jr.: "Courage confronts fear and thereby masters it."

I turn toward the heavy steel door and activate the intercom. The buzzer sounds and the lock clicks open, signaling the guard's arrival. Next stop: cell lockdown. I glance with pride at my new Fearbusters lining up to exit now. In their orange jumpsuits, twelve inmates are weaving their bright colors through this drab, windowless space.

Poetry
Chet Corey

How Wisely Made, the Wood Frog

I must remember that the wood frog,
who has buried himself
beneath the leaf pile I never got to
and has frozen as solid as the ice dam
on the shade side of our sagging overhang,
will thaw from the inside out—
heart first, not head first—
before his hind legs
lift him from beneath leaves in one leap . . .
then another . . . and another
until he enters at the open edge of pond
and finds again his song.

Poetry
Kathryn Knudson

Refuge

Silent words climb toward the ceiling.
Towering shelves filter an autumn
sunset while the scent of well-read

books comforts me. The rows open
to a clearing of abandoned oak tables,
chairs left haphazardly by minds

already onto the day's last errand or
drinks and laughter over shared jokes.
My only companion is the librarian

patiently restocking shelves, an
errant wheel whistling on his cart, a
persistent bird calling for a lost mate.

Creative Nonfiction
David J. Laliberte

Canada

Vivid are the colors of Minnesota's North Shore in October —all fluorescent yellows, oranges, burnished bronze. I'd never been this way before, so I was magnetized to the bus window, unable to draw my vision away. We passed the landscape quickly, zooming up Highway 61, but the flaming trees kept coming, unending, like waves in the biggest of lakes beyond.

We arrived at the arena, some nondescript place with incandescent lighting and gray-painted halls. But I prepared the same way as always: light jog 'til the first beads of sweat emerged from my brow, sluggish body warming like a bear in spring; tinny music from *Titanic* pulsing through the well-worn headset earpieces covered in a once-cushy foam; shin pads, terribly odorous, on left leg, then right. Soon we were on the ice, brisk wind through our face masks as we glided around an artificial pond.

What I remember then is perching in front of the net, my directed place as a defense man, tenseness, as usual, turning my legs into Lake Superior driftwood. Then my helmet came off, pulled from the back over my arched body like the violent shucking of corn. The bludgeoning began. In a fabric cave of darkness, jersey tangled about my head, I fell to my knees, a penitent disciple facing stones, and the warmth began spilling out of me. I never hurt, but I remember the silvery explosions on the screen of black before my eyes—all starry and lingering, like the glittery aftermath of a July firecracker. Raising my elbows in front of my face, I blocked one assault, a desperate shield over a fallen lamb, but then fireworks cracked again and again and again until the clanging gong that was my head rang out and out through the night.

Later, towel pressed against the remnants of my face, I sat in the vacant locker room, assistant coach unlacing my skates. "Let's see it," he spoke dryly, less a command than a question. I lowered the towel from my wounded visage and my one open eye beheld the cloth, all cardinal red, like those autumn sugar maples breezing past us on our bus ride north. The coach in front of me, a former Division III national champion who doubtless had seen many a scuffle and their accompanying crimson stains, cringed. I knew it must be bad.

A couple hours afterward, lying on a raised emergency room bed, I bantered with a suture-tying doctor.

"Ever been to Thunder Bay?" he asked.

"No, and I may not return," I replied, smirking. The physician's needle, dangling an inch or so beneath my right eye, pricked and tugged, pricked and tugged at my mostly anesthetized cheek, laying a railroad track in skin. "Will there be a scar?" I asked, slightly hopeful that my face might look a little tougher in the future.

"Hard to say," came the reply. "All depends on how it heals."

Fine with me, I thought, closing my eyes to avoid the glaring yellow hospital lamp that pierced my gaze like a blinding Northwoods sun through the trees; beneath my eyelids, an orange-red haze clouded my field of vision, the foggy stratosphere of the planet Saturn. Soon, the tiredness pursuing me for hours finally caught up. All was warm within me and around me, and I softened into my comfortable mattress like a petered-out hiker lying on moss, and fell asleep. I had arrived in Canada.

Poetry – Tarah L. Wolff Editor's Choice
Justin Watkins

Driftwood One-Matcher

August
Sleeping on dredge islands
Hot sands
Nights alive with river fowl

Tall grass hummocks
Gray lumber and driftwood
A humble altar
Southeast into rising sun

The boy in the tent
He is my outbreathing
I guard the door
This and all days

Soon I will call his name
Bring him to the fire
To the first light
And the singing cranes

Poetry
Arnie Johanson

The Nymph in My Garden

When I open the bedroom drapes
I see her. Made of colored air, she's
draped in layers of gossamer veils.
Blond hair floats down her back
as she glides barefoot through tomato
plants, pirouettes around bean poles
and sings to birds, who reply with happy
melody but keep their distance,
uncertain what kind of being she is.
MacDuff, my border collie, gave chase
one day. Her smile stopped him cold.
She only stays a couple minutes,
then casts a glance at my window,
tosses her hair, winks and evanesces
away, leaving me with just MacDuff
to chase my solitude.

Creative Nonfiction
Elisa Korenne

Crossing Borders II: East Africa 1997

I couldn't know that Ethiopia was about to invade Eritrea when I rode a rusty bus to a dilapidated guard shack on the border. I was traveling with two Canadian friends. Our bus ride had been crowded and bumpy and accompanied by the clucks of chickens that the woman behind me kept stuffed between her legs.

At the border, we stood on top of a brown hill and saw more of the same barren brown hills stretching uninhabited in all directions. We waited for a thin man to check our visas and stamp our passports. Two clicking thuds, and my Canadian friends were through to Eritrea. The guard examined my U.S. Passport and flipped between the picture page and the Eritrean visa I had picked up in Addis Ababa after three days of being shunted between embassy offices and waiting on endless despondent queues. The guard slouched against the faded wood and shook his head. "It's not valid," he said and handed it back to me.

My voice stuck in my throat, then came out squeaky. "I just got this in Addis Ababa. It's valid." There was no other transportation. If the bus and my friends went on without me, I'd be left alone on this barren hill between countries.

I slapped the passport down on the table and jammed my finger on the center of the official stamp. "I am an American citizen. I have a visa. I am entitled to enter."

"Not valid," the guard repeated, pushing the passport back.

I thrust it at him again. "I told you, I got this visa from the Eritrean Embassy in Addis Ababa three days ago." I swallowed. "If you don't let me through, I don't have any way to get home."

The guard lifted his hands in the air away from my outstretched passport, the universal gesture of "There's nothing I can do."

My hands began to shake. "If you do not allow me to travel with my friends, I will be stuck here."

The guard pushed my passport back toward me.

"Please," I said, almost crying.

The guard dropped his eyes.

I couldn't breathe. What would I do if I were stuck on the border with no way home?

Suddenly, with no warning, and no reason I could fathom, the guard opened an invisible door in the rickety plank wall of the guard shack and gestured me though. I gulped down my tears and entered a hidden office the size of a closet. At a large formal desk, I saw a bigger, more imposing man in a collared shirt and tie. I felt the sting of hope. I presented my passport and made my case again, my throat tight as a hatchet. The man said nothing. He flipped the pages of my passport back and forth. Then, handing the passport back to me, he nodded and gestured to the other wall where there was another door, the one that led across the border.

I walked through.

Poetry – Honorable Mention – Sharon Harris Editor's Choice
Brianna Liestman

Mugs

You know a person based on their coffee mug—
size, color, transparency, shape.

For instance, a large mug
indicates a high tolerance:
"This person can handle exactly twenty ounces
of bullshit."
A little mug indicates someone
prefers to enjoy life in small doses.

A clear mug is an open invitation
into someone's soul
while those who choose opaque mugs
prefer to keep their secrets.

But maybe I read too much into drinkware;
yet, as you sit across from me
in this café, I see
in your disposable cup
you are ready to leave any time
and my ceramic mug indicates
an intention to stay.

"The talking stick is a Native American tradition used to facilitate an orderly discussion. The stick is made of wood, decorated with feathers or fur, beads or paint, or a combination of all. Usually speakers are arranged in a talking circle and the stick is passed from hand to hand as the discussion progresses. It encourages all to speak and allows each person to speak without interruption. The talking stick brings all natural elements together to guide and direct the talking circle." —Anne Dunn

This year, we received over 370 submissions from 159 writers. From these, the editorial board selected 90 poems, 33 creative nonfiction, and 29 fiction pieces from 100 writers for inclusion in this volume.

Please submit again!

www.thetalkingstick.com
www.jackpinewriters.com

Contributors

Without the following contributors, this Talking Stick would not have been possible. Thank you to everyone!

Benefactors

Paisley Kauffmann
Sonja Kosler
Harlan and Marlene Stoehr
Marilyn D. Wolff

Special Friends/Single

Frances Ann Crowley
Mike Lein
Joni Norby
Cathy Wood

Good Friends/Couple

Faith and Dan Sullivan

Good Friends/Single

Marlys Guimaraes
Pagyn Harding
Deborah Rasmussen
Candace Simar
Peggy Trojan
Steven R. Vogel

Friends/Single

Sharon Chmielarz
Chet Corey
Shirley Greves
James Robert Kane
Ronald j. Palmer
Joel Van Valin
Susan Niemela Vollmer
Cheryl Weibye Wilkie

Niomi Phillips $50 pledged in the name of Louise Bottrell

Author List

Beverly Abear
Pagyn Alexander
Olivia Anderson
Lina Belar
James Bettendorf
Louise Bottrell
Mary Lou Brandvik
Janice Larson Braun
Tim J. Brennan
Stephanie Brown
Sue Bruns
Judy Budreau
Sharon Chmielarz
Jan Chronister
Mary A. Conrad
Chet Corey
Sarah Cox
Frances Ann Crowley
Dianne M. DelGiorno
Norita Dittberner-Jax
Charmaine Pappas Donovan
Carol Dunbar
Virginia Eckert
Larry Ellingson
Edis Flowerday
Marsha Foss
Cindy Fox
Neil Millam Frederickson
M. E. Fuller
Katie Gilbertson
Georgia A. Greeley
Annamae Gunsolus-Holzworth

Marlys Guimaraes
Richard G. Hagen
Kate Halverson
Laura L. Hansen
Sharon Harris
Audrey Kletscher Helbling
Jennifer Hernandez
Arnie Johanson
Charles Johnson
Christina Joyce
Meridel Kahl
Paisley Kauffmann
Karla Klinger
Norma Thorstad Knapp
Kathryn Knudson
Elisa Korenne
Janet Kurtz
David J. Laliberte
Kim A. Larson
Kristin Laurel
Mike Lein
Brianna Liestman
Renee Loehr
Dawn Loeffler
Linda Maki
Cheyenne Marco
Dan McKay
Susan McMillan
René Bartlett Montgomery
Michael Kiesow Moore
Marcia Neely
Ryan M. Neely

Author List

Joni Norby
David Eric Northington
Andrew O'Kelley
Alberta Lee Orcutt
Ronald j. Palmer
Yvonne Pearson
Susan Perala-Dewey
Alan Perry
Adrian S. Potter
Deborah Rasmussen
Kit Rohrbach
Lane Rosenthal
Deb Schlueter
Mary Schmidt
Ruth Schmidt-Baeumler
Lisa M. Bolt Simons
Peter Stein
Doris Stengel

Marlene Mattila Stoehr
Carissa Jean Tobin
Alberta Tolbert
Peggy Trojan
Steven R. Vogel
Beth L. Voigt
Susan Niemela Vollmer
Kim-Marie Walker
Justin Watkins
Elizabeth Weir
Bonnie West
Cheryl Weibye Wilke
Florence Witkop
Marilyn D. Wolff
Tarah L. Wolff
Kevin Zepper
Darryl Zitzow

www.ingramcontent.com/pod-product-compliance
Lightning Source LLC
Chambersburg PA
CBHW060743050426
42449CB00008B/1296